"As I was reading this wonderful book, my mind kept visiting the verse that seems to turn Jesus into a 'tumbleweed': 'Foxes have holes and birds of the air have nests, but the Son of Man has no place to lay his head' (Matthew 8:20). But if you follow Hilburn's sense of 'rootedness,' Jesus was never homeless. He built a home and drew others into their eternal home wherever he went."

— LEONARD SWEET,
author of *Soul Tsunami*, *Soul Salsa*, and *AquaChurch*

SETTING DOWN
Roots

LEAVING BEHIND THE TUMBLEWEED LIFE

Eddie Hilburn

NAVPRESS®

BRINGING TRUTH TO LIFE

OUR GUARANTEE TO YOU

We believe so strongly in the message of our books that we are making this quality guarantee to you. If for any reason you are disappointed with the content of this book, return the title page to us with your name and address and we will refund to you the list price of the book. To help us serve you better, please briefly describe why you were disappointed. Mail your refund request to: NavPress, P.O. Box 35002, Colorado Springs, CO 80935.

The Navigators is an international Christian organization. Our mission is to reach, disciple, and equip people to know Christ and to make Him known through successive generations. We envision multitudes of diverse people in the United States and every other nation who have a passionate love for Christ, live a lifestyle of sharing Christ's love, and multiply spiritual laborers among those without Christ.

NavPress is the publishing ministry of The Navigators. NavPress publications help believers learn biblical truth and apply what they learn to their lives and ministries. Our mission is to stimulate spiritual formation among our readers.

ISBN 1-57683-621-5

Cover design by The DesignWorks Group: David Uttley
Cover image by Photonica
Creative Team: Chris Seay, Steve Parolini, Darla Hightower, Arvid Wallen, Laura Spray

Unless otherwise identified, all Scripture quotations in this publication are taken from the HOLY BIBLE: NEW INTERNATIONAL VERSION® (NIV®). Copyright © 1973, 1978, 1984 by International Bible Society. Used by permission of Zondervan Publishing House. All rights reserved. Other versions used include: THE MESSAGE (MSG). Copyright © 1993, 1994, 1995, 1996, 2000, 2001, 2002. Used by permission of NavPress Publishing Group; the Holy Bible, New Living Translation (NLT), copyright © 1996. Used by permission of Tyndale House Publishers, Inc., Wheaton, Illinois 60189. All rights reserved.

Some of the anecdotal illustrations in this book are true to life and are included with the permission of the persons involved. All other illustrations are composites of real situations, and any resemblance to people living or dead is coincidental.

Hilburn, Eddie, 1964-
  Setting down roots : leaving behind the tumbleweed life / Eddie Hilburn.-- 1st ed.
    p. cm.
  Includes bibliographical references.
  ISBN 1-57683-621-5
  1. Community--Religious aspects--Christianity. 2. Christian life--Baptist authors. 3. Hilburn, Eddie, 1964- I. Title.
  BV4517.5.H55 2005
  248.4--dc22
                        2004024618

Printed in the United States of America

1 2 3 4 5 6 7 8 9 10 / 09 08 07 06 05

FOR A FREE CATALOG OF
NAVPRESS BOOKS & BIBLE STUDIES,
CALL 1-800-366-7788 (USA)
OR 1-800-839-4769 (CANADA)

*To Lisa, who without even trying stimulated the
most important root growing in my life.*

CONTENTS

ACKNOWLEDGMENTS

This book is more of an interpretive autobiography than a research project. The lens through which I interpret "root growing" is the lens of my own experience of rootless living. And while the process of helping others on this journey has painted an additional hue onto the lens, I possess no illusions to perfect sight from my perspective. I do hope in the reading you'll discover something new, or at least see something in a way you haven't before.

While I didn't approach this book as a research project, I did plenty of reading in preparation for the writing. I especially want to say how much the writing of Dr. Edward Hallowell educated and inspired me.

I also want to say "thank you" to those who have allowed your stories to be told in this book. A word of clarification to other acquaintances, friends, and family members who may wonder if I've written about them: If I've told your story, I've already asked you for permission to include it. The stories may *look* familiar—some are composites of typical things I hear from tumbleweeds—but if you're wondering if a particular story is about you (and I haven't already talked to you about this), the answer is "No, well, yes." No, it's not taken specifically from your life story. But, yes, it very well could be about your life.

I want to thank Chris Seay who saw potential in this project. The idea for this book came to me while driving all alone on a rural road. I wasn't trying to think of a book to write. I wasn't thinking about *anything* in particular. But after I wrote down some ideas, I asked Chris if he thought this was something. In my life Chris is the perfect person to ask. He always seems to know *if this is something.* Thanks, Chris, for encouraging me to pursue this project and for your help along the way.

I also want to thank the people at NavPress. I appreciate their willingness to work with this first-time author. I especially appreciate developmental editor Steve Parolini. Steve, thank you for your patience with me. And thank you for your hard work to make this project a success.

INTRODUCTION

Wind sweeps through the deserted street of a long-forgotten ghost town. A loose shutter bangs somewhere in the distance. Tiny dust tornadoes suddenly swirl to life, and then just as abruptly vanish. Right on cue, a tumbleweed appears—but this tumbleweed doesn't roll lazily by. Driven by gale-force winds, it bounces erratically, ricocheting first off one building, then another, relentless in its randomness and determined not to rest for more than an instant in its uncertain journey.

This tumbleweed is my life.

Growing up without roots, I was blown from place to place, powerless to take control of my life and begin a meaningful, self-determined existence. For a long time I didn't recognize my own rootless condition. When you grow up without roots, you think that tumbleweed living is normal. It may be common, but it is *not* normal. I believe God created us to grow roots. However, I can see how I became conditioned to think of tumbleweed living as normal. As a child, I instinctively began to grow roots, only to be uprooted at every turn.

I remember one of the best seasons of my childhood—it began in the first grade and continued halfway through my second grade year. My best friend was Tim Owens. His aunt, Mrs. Owens, taught our first grade class. During this season I attended a small country church with my grandmother every Sunday for an entire year. (I know I attended *every* Sunday because I received a "perfect attendance" certificate saying so.) I was sometimes the only person in my Sunday school class. My Sunday school teacher told me how great it was that I attended even when others didn't and I felt special—I felt *valued*.

It was also during this season that our family bought a home with acreage and a lake. I *loved* that place. I played in the woods. I built a teepee and pretended to be an early Native American living by my wit and skill as an outdoorsman. I helped my dad drain the lake so we could restock it with bass. Life was great. I enjoyed everything about my life. And I was secure.

Can you see the roots growing?

Halfway through my second grade year my parents told me they were getting a divorce. Life suddenly became ugly. Though they claimed they no longer wanted to be together, my parents' life *revolved* around their conflict. I became a tool in their fights or even the focal point of an argument. Amid this turmoil, my mom had several boyfriends—we lived with some. My dad evidently had several girlfriends, too. And by the end of second grade I had attended at least four schools. That's four schools just in second grade.

I was uprooted.

Toward the end of my second grade year my parents decided to try to make their marriage work. We moved from Louisiana to Georgia—to a small town of 300—so my parents could make a fresh start. It didn't take long to make friends during this season of my life—friends like Greg, Peter, Byron, and Ronnie. (We were all in the gifted and talented class.) My friends and I spent entire summers in spontaneous adventure mode. We rode our bikes all over town. We built tree houses and shot BB guns.

Good performance at school provided me with a sense of belonging and accomplishment. Living on a farm/ranch also gave me plenty of opportunities to define myself. I learned to grow a garden, work with cattle, and ride a horse. My dad was instrumental in beginning a horse-riding club in our community. The club built a riding arena where we would have horse shows on Saturdays. I held the best barrel-racing time for kids under twelve. My life stabilized.

Can you see the roots growing again?

And then, at the beginning of seventh grade, my roots were once again torn from the soil: My parents told me that they were getting a divorce. This cycle of "grow roots for a while, then suddenly rip them out" defined my growing-up years. Pain and disillusionment followed on the heels of connection and hope.

Perhaps you know this tumbleweed life cycle.

Today, I am a pastor. I encounter many tumbleweeds in this role—tumbleweeds like Tim. Tim grew up in an urban community with alcoholic parents who had little involvement in his life. He excelled in academics and athletics, yet Tim's parents were so uninvolved in his life that not once did they see him play a little league baseball game or a junior league basketball game. After his parents divorced, Tim's mother became even more distant. She provided little guidance or boundaries. Tim will tell you that he raised himself.

Tim never learned to make vital and lasting connections with other people—he never learned how to accept care or extend care to others. He determined early in life that he didn't really *need* anybody to care for him. Today Tim is married to a wonderful woman and wants to have a meaningful marriage, and yet he doesn't understand her heart-cry that something's missing in the marriage. He can't see that what's missing is *him*. You see, Tim regularly forgets or neglects birthday celebrations and anniversary plans because of some other interest. And while he says he values his role as a father, he rarely sacrifices his personal agenda to help with the children.

You might think Tim is too self-involved. Perhaps he has yet to understand how important he is to his wife and children. Yet if you told Tim he needed to be more present with his family, he would say, "You're crazy. They don't care if I'm there or not.

What difference does it make?" It's never entered his mind that he has the capability to help someone feel special, important, or unique. He understands his practical value—earning money, mowing the lawn, and vacuuming the carpet. But he has no idea of his emotional and relational value.

I believe Tim wants to grow roots, but just doesn't know how. I'm convinced we're all relentless root growers. The long popularity of the TV sitcom *Friends* may be a window into this part of our souls. Have you ever wondered why *Friends* remained so popular for so long? Sure, the show was well-written with clever comedy and attractive actors. But there was something more—something that touched the heart of a tumbleweed. Imagine what it would be like to be friends with Chandler, Joey, Monica, Phoebe, Rachel, and Ross. You'd spend an inordinate amount of time together at Central Perk sharing life's joys and struggles. (Somehow that sofa would always be available for you and your friends.) Maybe you'd be as goofy as Joey, have a nerdy job like Ross, play and sing like Phoebe, or cook like Monica. Whatever your role, you would have a place and a people you could call your own. And you would grow deep roots there.

Friends was built using a similar structure to another TV success, *Cheers.* Instead of a coffeehouse or a communally enjoyed apartment, the *Cheers* gang gathered in the familiar surroundings of the bar for which the series was named. Each week a cast of characters that included a washed-up baseball player, a naive, small-town bartender, a cranky waitress, a momma's boy mailman, and a severely underworked accountant named Norm related to one another in a manner that was compelling in its effortlessness. When Norm would walk into Cheers, his predictable, "Hello everybody," was always followed by a refrain of "Norm!" spoken in unison by everyone in the bar. I wonder how it feels to walk into a place where everyone knows and accepts you.

The success of *Cheers* and *Friends* came from something more than good acting or good writing. These shows met a need in our souls, a need to connect.

This is the same reason I still love to watch *The Andy Griffith Show*. If you're familiar with the characters you know that Andy is the wise, competent, benevolent sheriff and that Barney Fife is the self-inflated bumbler who somehow is able to keep his job as deputy. I think I watch this show because I want to be Andy. I also watch because I'm afraid I may be Barney. Ultimately I watch because I know that either way, there'll be a place for me in Mayberry. If I'm Andy, Barney, or even Goober the mechanic, I can safely grow roots in Mayberry. In some ways I've spent my life looking for Mayberry.

I want to grow roots. I believe my friend Tim yearns for a rooted life. Perhaps you do, too. This book unveils my attempts to grow roots and live a purposeful existence. It also captures the truths I've uncovered as a spiritual leader walking alongside others yearning to escape the tumbleweed life. And it offers some intentional, practical decisions we can make to help our families grow strong, deep roots that support lives of real substance.

If you're a tumbleweed I invite you to journey with me. Even if you're not, you probably still know a tumbleweed or two. This book can help you understand the tumbleweed life—what it means to be rootless and what it takes to grow deep, lasting roots. Perhaps you're a leader in a position of influence. This book can help you counsel in the art of growing roots.

My goal is simple. Through these pages I want you—and those you love—to discover how to set down roots.

To find Mayberry.

Part One:
The Tumbleweed Life

Chapter One

CAN YOU SEE MY ROOTS?

During the spring of my third grade year, our family planted a garden in the usual garden spot. After a couple of weeks I noticed tomato plants growing in places where we didn't plant them—"volunteer" tomato plants, we called them. Seeds that once sat dormant in the soil had germinated and grown into small-yet-promising plants.

I decided I'd transplant these randomly scattered tomato seedlings to more suitable locations in the garden. I had no prior experience with transplanting, so I took the simplest and most direct method: I wrapped my fingers around the stem of each plant near the base and—one by one—decisively pulled them upward. I placed the dangling roots of the plants into small, carefully excavated holes and covered them with dirt, then packed the soil firmly around the stems. After each baby plant had been successfully relocated, I paused to admire my work.

A couple days later I returned to our garden to see how my transplanted tomato plants were doing. To my surprise and dismay, I discovered they had all died. And in that discovery,

I learned my first significant lesson about roots: Living things pulled out from their source of strength, from the soil that feeds them, often fail to thrive—and sometimes don't even survive. When *people* are pulled out from essential connections to family, friends, values, spiritual foundation—when they're abruptly transplanted—they often fail to thrive as well.

According to psychologist Archibald Hart, "Connectedness is essential to a healthy self. We must be connected to [God], connected to absolute values like honesty and goodness, connected within ourselves and connected to others."[1] Connecting in these ways deepens life's meaning and purpose—it helps to grow healthy roots to keep us from withering like my hastily transplanted tomato plants.

Tumbleweeds often lose their connectedness. Perhaps you know this feeling too—this lingering sense that "something's missing" in your life. I knew it well.

Connection to Family

I lost the connections with my family for a variety of reasons. My parents' rocky marriage finally ended in divorce when I was in seventh grade. The strain of their relationship made it nearly impossible for me to connect with my father's family. Every time I went to visit my grandmother, one of my aunts or uncles would download a boatload of disparaging comments about my mother or me. I never really felt welcomed at my grandmother's home after my parents' divorce. I don't blame her for that, and I know that she, too, mourned the loss of our relationship. Every one of us experienced a great deal of pain during that time. Thankfully, I have recently reconnected with her. I think she's as glad as I am about reestablishing the lines of relationship.

I lost both my parents when they divorced. My father's unfaithfulness was the most direct cause of the split, and since my mother had custody of my brother and me, that meant I had little contact with my dad. A greater loss, though, was that my dad had ceased to be the person I wanted him to be. I wanted him to be my hero. I wanted a dad I could honor and admire. I lost that dad. But unlike many children, who, over time and at the *right* time, come to realize their father isn't Superman after all, I lost my dad with one swift blow as he traded our family for selfish pleasure. When my dad was killed in a rodeo accident during my eighth grade year, all hope of a meaningful connection with a father vanished.

I lost the vital connection with my mom in similar fashion. Hey, if my dad couldn't be honorable then at least I had my mom, right? Perhaps she would be the parent I could honor and admire. Wrong. My mom shared equally destructive moral failures that embarrassed me and, more importantly, isolated me from her.

There were some opportunities for me to develop connections with my mother's extended family. I lived near enough to have meaningful relationships and occasionally we would meet for family gatherings. Yet I soon discovered that even these connections could not last because of the dysfunction in the family relationships. Every family get-together became an arena for another argument or fight; every Christmas, a game of "which family members wouldn't show up?" because of ongoing feuds. We rotated alliances depending on whom we were angry with at the time. Long-term connections proved to be impossible. (Time, accompanied by growth, does heal wounds, however. And today I'm finding that the connections to my extended family can exist and even grow. I now run a direct line to these important people in my life, no longer needing to connect through my parents. I take ownership of these relationships and value them.)

This same tumbleweed condition of a loss of connection to family is evident in the colorful life of conman Frank Abagnale (as told in the book and movie *Catch Me If You Can*). Frank's father, Frank Sr., had swept the woman of his dreams off her feet in a village in France during World War II. After he brought her back to the States, he became a successful businessman *and* the model of the perfect dad. Frank's mother embodied the romantic ideal of a loving wife and mother.

Until the divorce.

After his parents split up, Frank's father lost the business and suffered a permanent and devastating blow to his morale. Frank Sr.'s desperate attempts to woo back his bride appeared as weakness. Desperation turned to defeat when she married his friend and associate. Young Frank Jr. was suddenly disconnected from the life he had grown to love and depend on—he became a tumbleweed, and eventually, a crafty crook who would elude the authorities for many years.

The ancient Hebrews understood and believed in the value of family connections. Look at how they describe the process of passing traditions to the next generation. "Repeat them again and again to your children. Talk about them when you are at home and when you are away on a journey, when you are lying down and when you are getting up" (Deuteronomy 6:7, NLT). Did you see it? The Hebrews simply assumed that parents and children would have close connections. They assumed that parents would talk to their children. They assumed families would take journeys together. *Of course* families would say good night together and rise to meet the new day together! These connections were critical for passing on faith and everything else essential to the next generation, so there was never a reason to question them.

The family connection is so important that Archibald Hart boldly states, "If an adult cannot answer the question 'Who am

I?' satisfactorily, it will be because the parents have failed to teach the child who he or she is."[2] According to attachment theorists, the nature of the attachment a child has with his or her parents determines the child's ability to confidently explore his or her environment. If a child feels insecure in either the environment or the connection to the parent, that child will be unable to act with confidence. A solid connection to parents provides a secure base that allows children to become adolescents who relate to peer groups, and eventually adults who relate not only to peers but also to spouses. The roots you grew in your relationship with your parents directly impact your ability to grow rooted relationships in every other context.[3]

Connection to a Community

Tumbleweeds often lose more than a connection to family—they lose a connection to community. Gail is a woman in her late sixties. She describes her father as a wanderer, and indeed, he moved the family many times during her childhood. They moved not just from town to nearby town, but from one region of the country to another—from rural Texas to urban southern California. Even more amazingly, sometimes Gail would leave for school from one house and come home to a *different* house—the result of her mother's constant search for a better place to live within the chosen town. Gail was forced to adjust quickly to a new neighborhood with new neighbors and new friends to make. However, she never felt secure enough to grow roots in any of the communities where she lived. Her experience served as a warning that they could move at any moment and she knew that each move would tear away any growing tender roots. It wasn't worth the effort to develop any real friendships. Gail knew the work and vulnerability required to grow relationships would be wasted.

I've heard a similar story from others as well—stories of parents chasing better jobs and more money; stories of parents bounced around due to financial instability; stories of parents who choose highly mobile careers in the military—or even the pastorate.

The loss of community is often at the core of that "something missing" tumbleweeds feel. That may be because people live *best* in community. We can look back to the Creation account to find the basis for this assertion. I make no assumptions about knowing every aspect of what it means to bear the image of God, but one facet of that image informs this idea of community. Consider Genesis 1:26-27:

> *Then God said, "Let us make man in our image, in our likeness. . . ." So God created man in his own image, in the image of God he created him; male and female he created them.*

When God created humans he didn't stop at one and declare everything "just fine." He created a *pair* to live in community. God then commissioned this pair to expand their community over the face of the earth. "God blessed them and said to them, 'Be fruitful and increase in number; fill the earth. . . .'"[4]

Theologian Stanley Grenz states, "God is 'community.'"[5] When God said, "Let *us* make man in *our* image" the only possible outcome was for God to create man as *them.* Doesn't this somehow match up with your own experience? What would it mean if *God is community*? Could that mean we are wired to *live* as a community?

If you have been disconnected from a sense of community you may identify with the comic strip *Betty*. In one episode, Betty and her workmates, Bea and Alex, search through the images on a "Where's Waldo" picture. Suddenly Alex exclaims, "There he is—behind the column." Bea and Betty walk away with the search completed. But Alex ponders a deeper thought, "Yep, I have no trouble finding Waldo. It's myself I can't find." All those tumbleweeds who've lost their community can resonate with Alex's insight.

Connection to Values

In *Catch Me If You Can*, Frank Abagnale Jr. lost something else besides his "perfect home" the day he walked into the house to find another man coming out of his parents' bedroom. He lost his connection to values.

The tumbleweed tale of Frank Abagnale Jr. could have been much different. Birth into the Abagnale household didn't necessarily destine Frank for a life of crime. In fact, after hours of evaluation utilizing written and oral tests, truth-serum injections, and polygraph tests, a University of Virginia criminal psychiatrist concluded that Frank Abagnale possessed a very *low* criminal threshold. Can you believe that he was an unlikely candidate for his years-long crime spree?[6]

Frank's escapades differed greatly from the life example of his father. Frank describes his father as "honest as the day is long, didn't have much of an ego, and was a hard worker."[7] So, what happened to Frank Abagnale Jr.? Frank says that his parents' divorce completely changed his life. He thinks he never would have taken the tumbleweed tumble if his family had stayed intact. Somehow when Frank's parents divorced, he lost the values his father had modeled for him—values which, until the divorce, were inherent in his personality.

Many tumbleweeds identify with this quote:

> *When I want to do good, evil is right there with me. . . .*
> *What a wretched man I am! Who will rescue me from*
> *this body of death?* (Romans 7:21,24)

When tumbleweeds experience disconnect from family and community they also lose a connection with their values. This doesn't mean that rootless people fail to understand the rightness or wrongness of certain actions. It means that they fail to act in ways that are consistent with the values they know to be true.

Lawrence Kohlberg identifies six stages of moral development. He theorizes that moving from one stage to another requires a certain amount of intellectual ability and maturity. Kohlberg states that morality includes reasoning, and without the ability to reason at the next level, one can't move to the next level of moral development. He also includes a social component that is required to move to the next stage of moral development. Without this social component, a person may be able to reason that certain behaviors are right or wrong but they can't actually behave in ways that are consistent with their reasoning. Kohlberg defines parents as one of the most important social factors in helping children develop morally.[8]

A group of thirty-four children representing a cross-section of a small Midwest town's socioeconomic makeup was the focal point of a study on the relationship between home life and values. Researchers found some of the children to be amoral and unable to control their emotions or their behavior. These children felt guilty for their behavior but were powerless to control themselves. In studying these children's home lives, researchers found families that were unloving, insecure, and inconsistent in discipline.

Researchers classified another group of children as expedient. These children "took the easy way out." Lacking a moral guide within themselves, they would do whatever was necessary to get along within the social context and to experience as much pleasure as possible. It was discovered that expedient children's parents had a laissez-faire style of relationship with them, drew few definite boundaries, and approved of the children in general ways.

Some of the children fit into the "conforming" category. Though hostile, they contained their hostility by means of a guilty conscience. Their depressed, dull moods kept them from standing up to the world. Their home lives were described as autocratic and punitive. Trust was not a characteristic of the relationship these children enjoyed with their parents.

Researchers described the children with the highest level of morality as rational-altruistic. These children possessed firm, internalized moral principles and applied these principles to various life situations. They had respect for themselves and others and exuded self-confidence. It's probably no surprise that these children came from homes where parents displayed regular approval for the children and harmonious loving relationships were the norm.

This study may prove to be insightful for tumbleweeds. While it highlights the importance of a rooted relationship with your parents, it also reveals the moral deficiencies of those who never enjoy that rooted relationship. The children who connected emotionally to their parents in a secure environment developed clearly defined value systems that they owned and followed. Without that connection it is certainly possible to learn right from wrong, but much more difficult to behave in ways consistent with that knowledge.

Steve's parents divorced when he was a preschooler. His mother remarried twice. Her first choice turned out to be a man who physically abused her, and the third husband was an alcoholic whom she later divorced as well. By the time Steve entered high school he maintained no active contact with a father and no secure emotional contact with his mother.

At eight years old Steve began riding a bus to a local church every Sunday. Steve grew to love not only the people who drove the bus but also the adults who taught Sunday school. As a result of the care of these adults, Steve joined the church.

When Steve got older, he began helping with the bus route. On Saturdays he would visit the children, as church members had done with him years before. On Sundays, Steve would go door-to-door collecting the children and helping them onto the bus.

None of Steve's high school friends knew of his involvement at church and certainly not his leadership in the bus ministry. No one would have ever guessed that Steve even *attended* church. Peers at his high school knew Steve as the guy who used the most obscene language, the guy who bragged about sexual exploits, and the guy who was the life of many parties. With a drink in hand Steve provided all the entertainment any party needed.

If you could look inside Steve at this time in his life, you would probably have seen a set of values very different from what his behavior suggested. Without a rooted relationship with his parents, Steve lost his connection to his values. His involvement at church had certainly given him the information he needed to make good decisions. But the disconnection from his parents had disconnected him from an ability to behave in ways consistent with what he knew to be best. Today as an adult, Steve works to connect his lifestyle to his Christian faith in a meaningful way.

Connection to a Heritage

Many tumbleweeds have a difficult time answering the question "Where do you come from?" Have you ever thought about the importance of this question?

Former New York Giants head football coach Jim Fassel and his wife discovered that she was pregnant when they were attending college and unmarried. On April 5, 1969, they put up their infant son for adoption. Colorado laws prevented the Fassels or their son from finding one another.

When the laws changed many years later, John Mathieson began a search for his birth parents as the Fassels also looked for him. On Mother's Day 2003, the thirty-four-year-old John Mathieson first spoke to his birth parents. John said, "I just lost it and cried for two hours straight." He told *Today Show* cohost Matt Lauer that he had thought of his birth parents every day for years.

John Mathieson loves his adoptive parents very much and they love him. He is happily married with a family. He has a good job and an enjoyable life. So why did John experience such emotion in finding his birth parents? Why had he wondered about them every day?

Because he needed to know where he came from. We all need to know where we come from. Some tumbleweeds have lost the connection to their heritage. Even if it is less than ideal, a heritage—a clear understanding of "where we're from"—gives roots a place to grow.

Connection to Spirituality

Spirituality is often another broken connection for tumbleweeds. Some have never learned what it means to have a relationship with God. But many more—in their efforts to find a larger purpose, to find roots—try on religion, only to discover that participating in religious activities religiously doesn't equate with experiencing a spiritual connection. I've seen this pattern in some of the people I work with. They chase religion—ritual and routine—in hopes that they'll grow spiritual roots, but they miss out on growing a relationship with God.

In the movie *Signs*, Mel Gibson plays Episcopalian priest Graham Hess. While driving his car through the countryside one evening, he comes across an accident scene. The already unsettling scene turns tragic when Hess discovers his wife is a victim of the wreck — and near death. Hess administers last rites to his wife as she loses her life on the side of the road. But something at the accident scene affects Hess deeply, forcing him to question God as well as his own calling as a priest. In response to his doubts, Hess resigns as Newtown's reverend and returns to farming in Bucks County. His questions multiply and his crisis deepens when crop circles appear on his farm.

In a pivotal scene in the movie, Hess wonders aloud about the reality of God: "You just have to ask yourself, what kind of person are you? Are you the type that sees signs? Sees miracles? Or do you think that people just get lucky? . . . Is it possible that there are no coincidences?" Ultimately, Hess sees the signs that answer enough of his questions for him to believe once again. He rediscovers that life has purpose and that God cares. Like us, Hess needed more than religion. More than ritual or routine, he needed a spiritual reconnection — a relationship with God Himself.

Connection to Ourselves

Some of us have lost a connection to ourselves. We have spent so much energy tumbling and resisting the winds that we have never defined who we are. We've worked hard to establish a coherent, unshakable appearance and yet remain hollow. We are like a basketball with a slow leak, regularly pumping ourselves up so no one notices our emptiness.

We wish we could be more like a bowling ball — solid and consistent all the way to the core. A bowling ball would have so much more impact. Hold a basketball and a bowling ball at shoulder height and drop them into a sandbox. Watch your toes! Which one makes the greater impact?

The winds often attempt to define tumbleweeds. One wind pushes me toward the latest clothes, cars, and gadgets and tells me I'll find significance there. Another wind blows me toward defining myself by my job and chastises me if I don't sacrifice everything to advance my career.

A connection with myself — with who I am — supplies me with resources to resist the winds. If I allow them to define me I will be blown in every direction. I can choose instead to define myself — a bowling ball isn't easily blown across the yard.

The other day I was doing my usual spring cleanup. As I pulled weeds out of the flowerbed I came to a dead plant. I planted this thing last spring and it was supposed to grow into some kind of perennial flowering bush. Evidently the winter had been too hard on it and now it had died. I felt disappointed. I had imagined enjoying the beauty of the colorful blooms for a long time.

Disgusted at such a frail specimen, I grabbed it by the base and started to pull. It didn't come out easily. I pulled harder. Finally, the soil gave way and I dislodged the source of my frustration. Wanting to show my contempt I took a closer look at the plant's roots. They weren't brittle. They weren't dead. They were supple and full of life. Then I noticed what I hadn't seen before: a little sprig of green was growing just at the base of the plant.

The plant wasn't dead after all. It had just gone dormant. By going dormant, this survivor had endured the winter. The growing roots were still hanging on. I gave up too soon. If I'd just waited and nurtured the plant a little I could have enjoyed its beauty for a long time.

Don't make this mistake. Don't give up too soon. You may still have roots that are hanging on. You've endured the winter and now you're ready for the world to enjoy the beauty of the person you were meant to be.

Chapter Two

THE LONELY WAIL
OF THE TUMBLEWEED

The winds of an unsettled life blow tumbleweeds from place to place, bouncing them from one new experience to another. Sometimes a new place excites tumbleweeds. New things excite all of us to some degree. New jobs, new houses, new friends, new spouses. Thanks to the influence of Madison Avenue, we automatically associate *new* with *improved*. New *must* be better. New *is* often better—for a while. But the satisfaction that follows the excitement is short-lived and, eventually, a familiar yearning returns. It's in these moments between the old new thing and the next new thing that we realize the sad song we've been hearing off in the distance is coming from us. We don't hear it often because it's so easy to drown out the sound with the exhilaration of something new. But what if we stopped to listen? What if we paused to embrace the pain? *Our* pain.

The movie *Good Will Hunting* tells the story of a

disconnected young man learning to connect. Early on in the story, the troubled Will Hunting (played by Matt Damon) is ordered by the court to meet with a counselor, Sean Maguire (played by Robin Williams). Will doesn't want to be there and makes it perfectly clear to Sean that the counseling will be a waste of time. It isn't until Will finally admits the existence of terrible pain that he clears the first hurdle toward healing.

Admitting the existence of pain is an important step toward learning how to grow roots because that pain is often the very result of rootlessness. Karen learned early to cover the pain of family upheaval. As a child she drew idyllic pictures of her family. She included everyone with great attention to detail—mother, father, eight-year-old brother, and six-year-old sister. The brightly dressed family stood close together with broad smiles across everyone's faces. Even the family cat grinned. Karen's drawings belied the painful angry divorce of her parents.

Adults sometimes believe that these drawings reflect the true feelings of the children. Karen's drawings more expressed her deepest wishes. More than anything she wanted her family to experience togetherness and peace. All the while, Karen felt more insignificant, alienated, and distrustful. Upon their divorce, her parents needed Karen to care for them. In the course of her caregiving, Karen lost her parents and her childhood. As a teenager, she hoped to one day marry and have children but she feared that the marriage could end in divorce. This fear made even the thought of marriage almost intolerable.[1]

Distrust

Some of us have developed a distrust that shades many, if not all, of our relationships. In the broad scale of things, we have lost trust in the basic structures of society. Obviously we don't trust government. Who would? The Camelot world of the Kennedys fell to the realities of sexual affairs and selfish ambition. "Ask not what your country can do for you but what you can do for your country." Right. The idealism of youth faded into the cynicism of reality. Vietnam. Watergate. And who can forget such classic lies as, "Read my lips . . ." and "I did not have sexual relations with that woman"? We have begun to think that politicians do their best work by providing material for late-night TV.

If we can't trust government, then what about business? One word—Enron. Whether it's the historical truth or simply the way we'd prefer to remember things, it seems companies *used* to take care of their employees. Go to work for a company. Spend your life giving them at least forty hours per week. The company will do everything it can to continue to employ you and will even provide a retirement plan to take care of you when you can no longer work. Today, that kind of employer/employee relationship is the exception, not the norm. Many employees feel that the companies they work for don't care about the employees—benefit cuts and "workforce reductions" are far more common than twenty-five-years-of-service retirement parties. And after the scandals we've witnessed, who would believe that companies really were interested in their employees, or for that matter, the stockholders?

Okay, I've shot down government and big business. What's next? Religion? Religion is not immune to the gaze of cynicism. We have watched religious radicals fly airplanes into skyscrapers filled with people. We have learned of abortion clinics that have been bombed in the name of pro-life. True, any society has its fringe element that does not represent the whole. So is there some element of religion that can be trusted? Many are saying, "No." Cynics quote examples of systemic sexual abuse, infighting among those who call themselves brothers and sisters, and other abuses of control and shame.

Since God's representatives are taking it on the chin, so is God. But that doesn't mean society isn't hungry for spirituality. Tune in any afternoon and you're bound to hear Oprah talking about the spiritual nature of life. And a TV show that debuted in the fall of 2003, *Joan of Arcadia*, depicts a teenage girl who encounters God in the form of a different person every week. Amber Tamblyn, the actor who plays Joan, describes the show as not being so much about God, but about life and spirituality and beauty. If you look closely, our current search for spirituality is not really a search for God—it is more of a spiritual cafeteria. We take a little from this religion, a little of this spirituality, and add our own ideas. Cynicism toward religion has birthed a do-it-yourself spirituality—a culture in which we each can create our own God.

Creating our own God only leaves us more rootless. A custom-made God is a God for only one person—not a connection to a greater purpose. If we look carefully, we may also discover that our custom-made God is simply a mirror of ourselves. When this God fails to satisfy our deeper longings, we feel more alone than ever.

The loss of trust in these major societal structures—government, business, religion—unmoors us. We still desire rootedness, but we won't find it there. So we turn to the only place left to find it: our personal relationships. Even these are not immune to distrust.

In *Good Will Hunting*, Will meets a girl and falls in love with her. It's a familiar Hollywood story. But instead of embracing the love she desired to return to him, he pushed her away, unable to trust that she could actually love him. Will was living out what so many tumbleweeds know from their own experience: After being hurt by people who say they love you, it becomes difficult to trust that *anyone* will love you. These wounds can result in scars and calluses—scars that breed relational suspicion and calluses that lead to relational disorder. Both lead to shallow personal relationships—the kind that preclude the possibility for growing deep roots.

Alienation

Distrust leads to alienation. *Since I don't trust anybody or anything, I refuse to attach myself. I will avoid anything that might result in pain.* Pain avoidance separates us from anyone and anything that could anchor our lives and help provide meaning.

When I was a teenager my family life caused me a great deal of pain. I wanted a family that provided a safe place for me to be me; instead I felt abandoned and betrayed. I quickly learned that if I became vulnerable and open, I would experience more pain than it was worth to try to connect. As a result, I determined I would never need anybody else. I made a conscious decision to trust *myself* for everything.

Alienation is different from simply feeling lonely—it is a separation that leaves you *truly* alone. Separating yourself from others may protect you from pain, but it also removes you from the opportunity to experience a full, rooted life. What do you do to prisoners if you really want to punish them? You put them in solitary confinement. What's worse than being locked up for the rest of your life? Being locked up by yourself.

Some tumbleweeds have voluntarily chosen solitary confinement. We've emotionally locked ourselves up, built walls to separate us from the source of our pain. Yet those same protective walls also separate us from the nutrients we need to grow deep roots.

Anger often accompanies alienation. When she was a small girl, Becky lost her older sister to drowning. The two girls had been playing in and near a river after a heavy rain. Strong currents grabbed and swept the older girl away while Becky stood helplessly on the bank and watched.

Becky's parents never recovered from the loss of their oldest daughter. And they lost more than that. They lost the ability to show affection to Becky. They lost their will to parent Becky. In a matter of minutes, Becky had lost her sister, her parents, and herself. Alienation and anger began to take root inside Becky.

Becky's anger over the emotional separation from her parents reinforced her alienation. Though very successful today, Becky works alone. She plays golf alone. Her anger has sabotaged any intimacy that might have grown in her marriage. Her children avoid significant contact with her. She's never let down by business associates. She never needs to depend on teammates. Becky has discovered how to avoid further pain.

Becky has avoided pain, but at what cost? Is she happy and fulfilled? Hardly. Her life echoes with the hollowness of missing connections. And yet, even out of the cave of alienation, she desperately seeks something deep enough to really matter.

Insignificance

Some tumbleweeds are quite successful, at least according to the accepted standards of success—a good job, a nice home, more money coming in than going out. If you could look inside their hearts, you might be surprised to discover many think of themselves as insignificant. People who live isolated lives will always struggle to find significance.

As human beings we find significance in relationships with others. What's so bad about being on a deserted island? All the pictures of deserted islands I've seen look pretty good. The tropical environment is appealing. You don't have to dress up to go to work. You can sleep as late as you want. And you're bound to develop a fantastic tan. So what's the problem? It's a *deserted* island. You live alone.

In the movie *Cast Away*, Tom Hanks plays Chuck Noland—a FedEx worker who ends up stranded on one of these idyllic deserted islands. Did he crave connectedness during his years alone? Just ask his friend Wilson—a volleyball that he imbued with a personality in order to have a personal relationship with something, anything.

At one point in the movie, a dehydrated, exhausted Chuck risks his life to save Wilson, who has floated away from the raft into the choppy seas. *He risks his life to save a volleyball.* To Chuck, Wilson was more than a leather, air-filled ball. Wilson gave Chuck significance. Without Wilson, Chuck would have lost meaning.

There was another person who gave Chuck significance—the intended recipient of a FedEx package he salvaged from the plane wreck that had brought him to the island. This package, adorned appropriately with angel wings, gave Chuck another reason to live. It connected him with a real person "somewhere out there"—someone who needed this package. Without Wilson or the angel-winged package, Chuck would have despaired in insignificance. He would have lost hope.

I have come to believe I am an important person not because of what I do but because of who I am in community. Sometimes I play golf with people who say, "I have never had a lesson in my life, I taught myself to play," at which point everyone else is thinking, "I could have guessed that." Sure, golf is an individual game, but the best golfers in the world don't try to pursue the game by themselves. They gather the best teachers, trainers, and psychologists to help them improve.

People who say, "I need no one," will never find the same kind of significance as those who see themselves as part of a community. We can paint over feelings of insignificance with an air of confidence, a happy-go-lucky attitude, or a wall of defensiveness, but tumbleweeds take an important step toward rootedness when they admit that they really do need community.

The Need to Grieve

Tumbleweeds need to grieve. Does this surprise you? You've experienced loss—loss of trust, loss of connection, loss of identity, loss of security, and, ultimately, loss of rootedness. Don't hesitate to recognize the importance of these losses. The grieving process helps us to become more rooted.

Grief usually moves through predictable stages: shock, emotional release, depression and loneliness, physical symptoms of distress, feelings of panic, guilt, anger and resentment, resistance, and (hopefully) hope. Some people remain tumbleweeds because they get stuck in the grief process. Perhaps you're trapped at an identifiable roadblock.

If you are stuck, it may be because you hesitate to admit your loss—you never needed anybody anyway, right? The grieving process won't begin until you admit that you *do* need these people or these things and that you've lost them. Don't be surprised if this sense of great loss is accompanied by deep emotions. Go ahead and cry—losses like yours are painful.

At some point down the path of grieving, you'll spend time in the middle of anger and resentment. You may cry out, "Who uprooted me?" You may blame parents, extended family, culture, God, or all of the above. That's okay—it's normal to spend time here, but this is a place to move through, not a place to call home. Anger and resentment left unresolved will poison roots and create a shallow-rooted life. If you want to move forward, you'll need to resolve your emotions instead of allowing them to become embedded. But the next step isn't easy. Remaining in the resentment and anger may feel more comfortable to you than the alternative—the idea of reconnecting with others beyond the grief may even seem impossible. Push forward, keep at it—at the end of grief you will find hope.

A Glimpse of Hope

I want to end this chapter with a glimpse of that hope—and of the happiness it often brings. One of the defining characteristics of a tumbleweed existence is an absence of happiness, but that absence is not for the lack of trying. Many tumbleweeds allow themselves to be blown from place to place because they're on an unending search for happiness. They think, *I am not happy here. Maybe I will be happy over there.* Or there. Or perhaps there. They haven't discovered that happiness can be found right where they live. Happiness is not a destination. Happiness is what happens as we make certain choices along the journey.

I invited you to listen to the pain. I wanted you to stop and hear it, *feel* it. Recognizing that this pain is real can help you see that your current choices are not producing what you really desire. *If you keep doing what you've always done, you keep getting what you've always gotten.* I'm not suggesting that we avoid the kind of pain that accompanies a desire to do something good. Like exercise. Or studying to master a discipline. Or saying "no" to your children. I'm talking about the kind of pain in your soul that sounds an alarm. Your body contains nerve endings that tell you when physical pain is present—signals that warn you to stop certain activities or to avoid certain behaviors. Your soul also tries to tell you when pain is present. But if you're accustomed to rootless living—you count it as normal—you may have anesthetized your soul. Listen to the soul alarm. Allow the anesthesia to wear off, and as you feel the pain, you will know that this is not how life was meant to be.

I don't want you to think that pain and grief is the last song you will ever hear. Remember that hope is waiting at the end of grief. I want you to hear another song that lives in your heart. Maybe you haven't heard it in a long time—or at all. This song reaffirms our intense desire to grow rooted lives.

How can you hear the melody of this song? Start by remembering. Remember when this song was sung with loud abandon. You probably have some memory in your past; maybe in your childhood when life was the way it is supposed to be. It may be connected to a major event such as getting married or having a child. It is more likely something simple and ordinary.

In *The Childhood Roots of Adult Happiness* Edward Hallowell tells about a childhood snow day spent with his cousin Jamie and a toboggan on a hilly golf course. Together they experienced the tireless joy of time spent with a best friend laughing and losing all thought of anything else. Hallowell says, "That was as happy a day as I ever had."[2]

In *The Sacred Romance* Brent Curtis recalls a childhood memory of a favorite place to explore. After describing in great detail the magical location at the borders of the farm where he lived, he continues:

> *I remember being in that place until the music of life would fill me with the knowledge of some Romance to be lived; an assurance that there was a reason to joust against dragons with wooden swords; a reason to wear not one but two pearl-handled revolvers in the cowboy stories I weaved and lived out each day; a reason to include a pretty girl who needed to be rescued, even though I was far too busy fighting the bad guys to be captured by love. The magic assured me of loves and*

lovers and adventures to be joined and mystery to be pursued.

The Romance of that place would surround me as I rose and returned through the cornfields in response to my mother's distant call. It comforted me with a familiarity that seemed to connect me with things that were at once very old and still becoming new. Lying on my bed, with my parents far off downstairs in another part of the house and a geography of the heart I did not then know, I would fall asleep, romanced by some unseen lover that, back then, I only knew from those singers in the summer moonlight.[3]

These childhood memories of happiness share a common thread: a sense of connection. Ed Hallowell connects to his cousin and best friend through the shared experience of joy-filled abandon. The snow and the toboggan provided the opportunity, but the magic was in the connection. Brent Curtis's memories are painted on a canvas of connection. The very land on which he walked connected him to generations past. Knowing that he couldn't wander for too long without hearing his mother's voice connected him with a sense of security and importance. And falling asleep with the knowledge that mom and dad were in a room downstairs connected him with comfort and consistency. With these roots firmly implanted, connections to nature and even connections to transcendence became possible.

When I think back on my best childhood memories, one event stands out against the background. I was in fifth grade and we were living in that small town in north Georgia. On Saturdays we would participate in horse shows. My dad had always loved horses and he owned one named Booger. It's a strange name, I know. I rode Booger in barrel racing and other timed events. One Saturday our local riding club was hosting the horse show. That particular Saturday I won the barrel-racing competition for kids twelve and under. Not only did I win, I set a record for kids twelve and under. Nobody had ever heard of someone my age riding that fast. I rode faster than most of the adults had ever ridden.

What seals the memory as one of my best is my dad's response. He was amazed. He told me how great I had done. He told me I looked like a champion. My dad went around telling *everybody* about his son that day. One man wondered aloud if something might have been wrong with the timing device since his nephew ran such a slow race and I ran such a fast race. My dad simply laughed and told him that the timing device was just fine, said I was just a superior rider. Being accepted and affirmed by my dad was an intoxicating taste of the way things were supposed to be.

What is your happiest childhood memory? If you can remember a connection and a sense of real joy, the pain hasn't won. The melody of happiness still lives within your heart. Growing roots will allow the happiness to move from your memory into your present experience.

Chapter Three

THE WINDSTORM

*I*n October 1991, three storms combined to form the strongest storm ever recorded in history. Meteorologist David Epstein watched the storm unfold—or rather the three storms fold together—from a Hartford, Connecticut, TV station. As an old hurricane—Grace—was slowly dying out in the Atlantic Ocean, weather energy moving across the Great Lakes and a frontal system in New England converged on it. This combination reenergized the hurricane. Epstein watched something curious. Often multiple storms will compete with one another when they meet. But these storms *combined* forces. They cooperated to become the "perfect storm"—more officially known as "the Halloween nor'easter of 1991."

Winds blew across the ocean at 100 mph. Waves 100 feet high bashed the New England coast, destroying 200 homes. The Halloween nor'easter of 1991 killed nine people including six who had fished from the *Andrea Gail*—the ship featured in the George Clooney film *The Perfect Storm*.

The *Andrea Gail* was a 72-foot, steel-hulled swordfishing boat. Her crew reported by radio that they were fighting the storm in an attempt to make it through, but the storm was too strong. The crew and boat never made it home and were never heard from again. Rescue crews later found small parts of fuel drums from the *Andrea Gail*—but that was all they found. Interestingly, the *Andrea Gail* didn't even see the most violent part of the storm.

Sometimes I wonder if we live in the perfect cultural storm. Any single cultural change can have some impact, but when all the winds begin to blow at once, tumbleweeds swirl out of control. They're blown away.

The Winds

In his book *Bowling Alone*, Robert D. Putnam suggests that Americans have become less connected than ever before. They've lost connections with community, institutions, and each other.[1] The disconnection Putnam writes about is exactly what I mean when I use the term "rootlessness." The significant connections we need to derive meaning from life *are* our roots. When we lose these connections we essentially lose life's direction and purpose.

Signs of Disconnection

Americans have lost their ability to trust. During and after World War II, two-thirds of our nation believed that "most people can be trusted."[2] By 1964 that percentage reached an all-time high in the United States: 77 percent of Americans agreed that "most people can be trusted." We don't have a percentage for that question today, due to the different way polls are taken. But what do you think the percentage would be? How many today would say, "Most people can be trusted"? Do you keep the door to your home locked? Do you keep your car doors locked? Do you open the door to strangers? Do you think I am ridiculous for asking questions that have obvious answers? A time existed when people would have answered these questions quite differently. People who lived during that time would have also thought I was ridiculous for asking questions with such obvious answers.

Where there is trust, there is also reciprocity. I behave in certain ways toward others because I trust that someone will do the same for me. Yogi Berra put this more creatively when he reportedly said, "If you don't go to somebody's funeral, they won't come to yours."[3] This still exists today in the community where my brother Jeff lives. When he was diagnosed with a brain tumor, the people in his community came to the rescue. His friends volunteered to help him run his farm. People who regularly performed some service for him for pay wouldn't take money. The local farm and ranch supply store told him not to pay until his ordeal was over. The community even organized a calf-roping event to raise money and help his family.

My brother told me that where he lives people *have* to live this way. He said that if you drive by a farm and see someone who looks like he might need help, you stop and help. You do this because you care but also because you know that sooner or later you'll need someone to stop and help you. Jeff then asked me a stunning question. "Do people do these kinds of things where you live?" At the time I lived in one of the largest metropolitan areas in the country. I tried to make a few excuses but then had to admit, "No, *we* don't."

What do I do when I see someone who needs help? When I see someone on the side of the freeway with a broken-down car, I pass by. In the darker corners of my thoughts I wonder if they're faking the breakdown and instead are planning to rob me. Or worse, steal my car. In the more hopeful corners of my thoughts I rationalize a different way. "Surely they have a cell phone of their own and can call somebody to help." Either way, I convince myself it's not my problem. I'm usually in a hurry (when am I not?) and can't afford to stop. And then I finally land on this excuse: You can't help everybody who needs help.

A lack of trust partly explains our decline in political participation. In the 1960 presidential election between John F. Kennedy and Richard Nixon, 62.8 percent of eligible Americans went to the polls. In 1996, 48.9 percent of eligible voters went to the polls to choose between Bill Clinton, Bob Dole, and Ross Perot.[4] Consider the differences between those election times. In the 1960s, people generally trusted government. Three out of four surveyed during this time *disagreed* with statements such as "People like me don't have much say in government" and "Public officials don't care what people like me think." In the 1990s, that percentage had shrunk to one out of four.[5] Of course, you could blame a lot of that shift on the ripples that followed events between those two surveys such as Vietnam, the race riots, Watergate, and more. And if those events had an impact on trust, imagine how the subsequent political and big business scandals have impacted our ability to trust.

Reciprocity-producing trust makes a difference in all kinds of relational activities. If I trust that someone will invite me over to dinner, I will probably invite someone over for dinner. If I trust that someone will mow my lawn when I'm out of town, I'll probably mow someone else's lawn. I know what the Golden Rule says, "Do unto others as you would have them do unto you." It is truly a person of substantial character who is able to take the lead and do the first "good thing" for someone else. Most of us are much better responders than trailblazers. We treat others the way we expect to be treated. In a culture of distrust, that spells doom for all.

What about simply getting together with friends? A culture of healthy, growing relationships would be a positive sign that things are getting better, right? Sorry, more bad news. In 1975 the average American entertained friends at their home fourteen to fifteen times a year. By the end of the 1990s the average American entertained friends in their home eight times a year. That represents a 45 percent decline. Consider that the following activities—card playing, participating in a team sport, attending parties, and hanging out in bars—have also seen a significant decline. If this continues, it won't be long before we stop informal socializing all together. What happened to *Cheers* where "everybody knows your name"? Or *Friends* where everyone gathers in a common apartment or a local coffeeshop to talk? Apparently while we do enjoy watching people do this on TV, we don't actually participate in the activities as often in real life as we used to.

What Happened?

Putnam sums it up this way:

> *During the first two-thirds of the century Americans took a more and more active role in the social and political life of their communities—in churches and union halls, in bowling alleys and club rooms, around committee tables and card tables and dinner tables. Year by year we gave more generously to charity, we pitched in more often on community projects, and (in so far as we can still find reliable evidence) we behaved in increasingly trustworthy ways toward one another. Then, mysteriously and more or less simultaneously, we began to do all those things less often.*[6]

What were the conditions that made such a disconnection possible? What began to happen in the 1960s that caused us to become more disconnected? Why did our roots begin to atrophy? Putnam suggests several possibilities: *busyness, economic changes, changing families, mobility, suburbanization, the sixties revolution,* and *TV and other technology.*

Busyness

Almost everybody I know has the existential condition of busyness. I rarely find anyone who can honestly say, "I just have too much free time." (With the possible exception of senior adults who are confined to their home.) I know plenty of retired people who complain that they have so much to do they feel like they're back at work again—or that they'd rather be back at work when schedules at least had some consistency and familiarity. We live in an age marked by the emergence of time-management experts—people who offer us assistance so that we don't misuse any part of our day. We obsess about our planners and our Palm Pilots. But are people really busier today than they were forty years ago? We choose to be isolated and individualistic and fill our schedules with activities and actions that support that isolation. If my coffee cup is already full and you ask me if I want a refill, I say, "No thanks. Already full."

Research tells us that well-educated people are busier than they used to be. Both partners in a marriage often work—and they're working longer hours than they once did. Busy people rarely have the same time available to get together with people who would otherwise be good friends. My free time may not match your free time. But this is not enough to tell us why we are becoming more disconnected and rootless.

Economic Changes

Economic factors affect the way people interact. Putnam tells of a social psychologist who "found that the jobless became passive and withdrawn, socially as well as politically."[7] I have a friend who lost his job last year. Other than family, all of his social contacts came through work. After losing his job, my friend realized that he had invested much of his identity in his work. When he lost his job he nearly lost himself—he had tied his value as a person to his value as an employee. As he labored in looking for a new job, a sense of powerlessness began to take over. Why couldn't he make this happen? He felt disconnected and trapped, and helpless to do anything about it. Many of you who are reading this know just how my friend felt.

Changing Families

Years ago, when women began working outside the home, the shape of family life changed dramatically. This new dynamic impacted social contacts. Women who work full-time are less likely to entertain someone in their home, attend a club meeting or church activity, visit informally with friends, or volunteer for an organization. And their husbands are also less likely to entertain, attend church, or volunteer. Instead, many two-income couples spend their free time in activities that require little emotional or relational energy—they just don't have much left after a full workweek. This doesn't necessarily mean that if women (or men) stopped working outside of the home that they would choose connecting activities. Many choose to work *because* they would rather spend their time in their vocation than in relational activities.

Mobility

Mobility undermines connectedness. Even the anticipation of being uprooted makes us avoid connecting. People who expect to move in the next five years are less likely to vote, attend church, participate in clubs, or get in on a community project. And 40 percent of us expect to move in the next five years. Communities with high mobility rates are less connected. Higher residential turnover contributes to a general kind of unfriendliness. Crime rates are higher; schools perform more poorly; even longtime residents don't know their neighbors well.

The question remains, has mobility caused us to become less connected than forty years ago? The fact is that we may actually be less mobile today than forty years ago. Twenty percent of us moved every year in the 1950s. During the 1990s it was only 16 percent. We move less, but maybe *where* we move to is the issue. Instead of the frequency of the move, let's consider the destination.

Suburbanization

If you ask, you'd likely find most of your neighbors, friends, and work associates would be thrilled to find their own version of Mayberry. In reality, though, we are moving steadily away from Mayberry—into the suburbs. Putnam states, "In the 1950s barely half of all Americans lived in a metropolitan area, whereas in the 1990s roughly four of five of us did."[8] Through periods of urbanization our social connectedness thrived. But something different began to happen when we moved from urbanization to suburbanization.

When we moved to the burbs we started to segregate. Some of us moved behind walls into gated communities. We intentionally made a decision to keep others out of our lives. Yes, we stopped the door-to-door salesman, the criminal looking for an opportunity, and the Jehovah's Witnesses trying to convert us. But in the process we also fenced out the pop-in visitor and the unexpected guest. It's true that people theoretically could connect with one another inside a gated community. But do we? Not much. Most people leave and return to their home through an attached garage and don't even see their neighbors. Privacy fences surround our backyards. We've made it impossible to talk over the fence to a neighbor. We've walled ourselves in and others out. Some have called our behavior "cocooning." Cocooning is about as far removed as possible from connecting.

The Houston metropolitan area contains many master-planned developments. These developments attempt to create the image of "community." Sienna Plantation is one of those developments: *Living in Sienna Plantation means discovering, learning, and celebrating every day.* The literature goes on to say:

> *Welcome to Sienna Plantation—a thriving Fort Bend community filled with trees and nature, extraordinary amenities including the largest private water park in the South, championship golf, and multiple community options. It's a place where living and learning complement each other to the fullest, and celebration is the order of the day. Come visit Sienna Plantation.*

I want to visit. Don't you? Hey, I want to *live* there. But I do wonder how many of the Sienna Plantationers drive into their garage and don't see their neighbors. I wonder how many go to the water park and never have a conversation with another person—a person who may even be a next-door neighbor. I wonder how many people golf alone.

When Americans decided to live in a suburb they invented something called "commuting." The average American adult spends seventy-two minutes per day behind the wheel. We carpool less and utilize mass transit systems less and less. The next time you get stuck in a traffic jam, look around. You will see hundreds or thousands of people sitting alone all together. And what happens after that traffic jam? You begin a hectic day at work where someone expects more and more production from fewer and fewer people. Then you travel that same route home driving through another aggravating mess on the freeway. When you arrive at home do you feel like connecting? Are you interested in growing roots? Or are you hoping just to veg out in front of some TV show that requires nothing from your frazzled mind?

The Sixties Revolution

If the 1960s represented the height of connection as a natural part of life, then perhaps the crazy things that came about in the sixties pushed us over the edge. A break of trust played a major part in the revolution of the sixties and into the seventies. Can you trust a government that allows people who happen to be white to systematically degrade people whose skin happens to be black? And when someone did stand up to this inequality—when Martin Luther King Jr. shared his dream—someone killed him. John F. Kennedy articulated a new vision for America. Someone shot him, too. Someone was killing all of our heroes. Then, suddenly, we were thrown into the middle of a war in Southeast Asia. The government lied to us about the war. They lied about why we were there and how well we were doing. Many of us protested the war, but the government didn't listen. But they did shoot a few protestors on a college campus.

We decided not to believe anything the government told us. They told us drugs would harm us. We had to find out for ourselves. They said that sex . . . well, they didn't even talk about sex. Consequently, we started talking about it all the time. They fought against rock and roll. We celebrated it. They believed in short hair for guys. We grew ponytails. We revolted, and life would never be the same.

TV and Other Technology

Mass media has impacted us in ways we don't even realize, because many of us don't know what it's like to live without it. Many years before MTV, if you wanted to enjoy music you might turn on the radio, but you would be just as likely to gather at the town square or civic center for a community concert. Now you can just tune in or turn on for digital access to whatever kind of music you want, whenever you want it.

T. S. Eliot made an insightful observation about the early state of TV viewership: "It is a medium of entertainment which permits millions of people to listen to the same joke at the same time, and yet remain lonesome."[9] With TIVO I don't even have to listen to the joke when you do.

TV gives us a *virtual* community—but it still doesn't compare to real community. Millions of viewers probably felt like they were losing real friends when Monica, Phoebe, Joey, Ross, Chandler, and Rachel signed off the air in the final episode of *Friends*. But these characters were *not real people*. I know one woman who got overly involved in a *NYPD Blue* storyline. In one particular episode, viewers were left hanging when the show ended with a significant character in apparent grave danger. "Tune in next week to find out what happens" was the tease of this episode. So what did this woman do during the intervening week? She prayed for the characters in the show. Later, she admitted that she felt a little silly praying for characters on a TV show. But her action isn't that surprising. Like so many of us, she was *involved* in these people's lives.

In the virtual worlds provided by TV, viewers can experience community without the risks associated with reaching out to others. Little effort is necessary in the "relationship"—your commitment lasts only as long the show airs. But you also don't experience real community. The one-way relationships offered by a virtual community can never provide the community we really crave.

Over 75 percent of all homes in the United States have more than one TV, which means that family members can now each go to a separate room to watch in seclusion. Is that a good thing? TV also keeps us tied to our homes, distanced from any potential connecting opportunities outside the four-walled fortress. More and more we say we want to use our discretionary time to enjoy a quiet evening at home. But that is often code for "sitting in front of the TV, vegging." We don't always even have a particular show in mind to watch. We just sit in front of the TV and turn it on. Then we surf. But this kind of surfing is quite the opposite of the visceral, focused, in-the-moment experience of riding an actual wave. This surfing is a mindless, scattered experience. And while we flip through the 200 digital channels, pausing for a moment at images that look marginally interesting, we simultaneously complain that we have nothing to watch. TV is, in many ways, the epitome of an "anti-community" device.

Even more benign kinds of technology have changed our lives in ways we didn't intend or expect. Let me give one example. Somewhere along the path of industrialization, refrigeration was invented. Some genius uncovered a way to cool the air temperature and everyone said "ahhh" as they switched on their air conditioners. We should say "thank you" for that invention. But the law of unintended consequences also plays in here. Before refrigeration, people sat on their porches in the evening to take advantage of the cool air. You know that a lot of connections were made, neighbor-to-neighbor, because of our need to cool off. We no longer need to sit on our porches. I'll admit I'm not ready to trade in my AC. But we need to recognize that the great technological advances we've made have had their impact on our ability to find community.

So What?

Do you agree we're facing quite a storm? A gale-force challenge to our ability to connect and grow roots? We can't stop the wind from blowing. But we can make adjustments. I know that I have to be intentional at growing roots—at connecting with other people. A culture that considers Instant Messaging no different from a traditional over-the-fence chat will not automatically assist me in growing roots. I have to do some real work. (That's where we're going in the next chapters.)

We know this won't be easy. We may have to decide at times to swim upstream—to live a countercultural life. But finding connectedness—growing roots—will be worth it. Let's get started.

Part Two:
Setting Down Roots

Chapter Four

DISCOVER YOUR HERITAGE

ometimes people ask me, "Where are you from?" They ask the question innocently enough (I guess a lot of people ask and answer this question without much consternation). I usually struggle to find an answer. I was born in Pine Bluff, Arkansas. We then moved to West Monroe, Louisiana. When I was seven our family moved to Ila, Georgia. We moved back to West Monroe when I was twelve. After high school graduation I moved to Marshall, Texas, to attend college. Upon graduation from college I moved to Houston. I lived in the Houston area for longer than anywhere else, but now I live in a small town in East Texas. You tell me. Where am I from?

It might be easier to answer the question "*Who* am I from?" Everybody comes from someone. My eleven-year-old son and I were riding along in the car when he asked me a question about a specific person in our community. I responded with the statement, "He doesn't have a family." It didn't take but a second for him to correct me with these insightful words, "*Everybody has a family.*" He's right. Some may not know their families—

they might struggle with the answer to the question "Who am I from?" But everybody comes from somebody.

Where do you come from? Who do you come from? These two important questions are difficult for many tumbleweeds to answer. Yet tumbleweeds anchor themselves when they begin to find these answers.

Discover It

What do you know about your heritage? What corner of the world shaped the history of your ancestors? Your parents? Your grandparents? Do you know about your ethnic heritage? You do have a heritage. If you can do the hard work of mining for these answers, you may find treasures you never dreamed of.

I recently made contact with some of my extended family. In my attempts to reestablish contact, I visited first with my aunt. We talked about my need to find my roots and discover my heritage. She was saddened that I felt as if I had no roots. "You do have roots," she said. "You do have a heritage. You just need to find them." Her words may seem simple, but they're packed with wisdom. Discovering our heritage allows us to reconnect with existing roots. Sure, we may still choose to be intentional about growing new roots later, but this heritage of old roots can be instrumental in helping us to do that more effectively.

As I began to reconnect with my roots I discovered some amazing things. One of the most important things I found is that people really did care about me. I know that may sound trite or perhaps naive, but I truly wasn't aware that these family members wanted to know me and be involved in my life. I found roots I didn't even know I had. And one of the nice features of old roots is that the connections are already wired. I just needed to plug in, so I took my children to visit my grandmother, whom

I hadn't seen in ten years. After the visit my eleven-year-old son said, "Just a few weeks ago I didn't even know I had a great-grandmother. Now I know all about her."

Through stories from my grandmother and my aunt, I got to know my great-uncle Ford. Uncle Ford was a spiritual leader in his community. He spoke softly and deliberately. He never used unnecessary or careless words. Sometimes I wish I were more like Uncle Ford (usually just after I've spoken bluntly and with a great deal of emotion). Uncle Ford also wrote a weekly inspirational column in the local newspaper, and I'm looking forward to reading his articles. As I make a connection to my Uncle Ford, old brittle roots are softening and becoming new again.

Discovering your heritage may seem like an attempt to live in the past, but to the contrary it could actually serve as your key to the future. Let me explain. Ancient Christian art often used the image of a boat to represent the church and an anchor to represent "tradition." Think about an anchor for a minute. You probably know that an anchor can keep you from drifting or being blown away. It can also help you move purposefully—even in a storm. Seafarers call this practice *kedging*. During turbulent seas a whole host of sailors in a motor launch or whaleboat would haul the anchor of the ship as far as the chain would allow them, then drop the anchor from the small boat. The ship would winch forward and then they would repeat the process. It was a slow, labor-intensive process, but the anchor allowed the ship to move forward.[1]

Our tradition or heritage can play the same role as that anchor. It can give us the ability to move purposefully forward while staying securely connected. As you discover your heritage you do not have to live in the past; you can live *out of* the past. You can bring the rich resources of those who have gone before you into your life.

You may resist this aspect of growing roots in an attempt to avoid anything that could cause you more pain. But if you recast the painful memories, you can learn from them instead of relive them. This is possible only if you can take the frightening step of walking back into the past and looking at the pain with new eyes. That doesn't mean the pain will go away. But at least then, the pain will count for something. If you don't deal with the pain, it can cloud the way you see your past—your heritage—and the way you shape your future.

One critical key to dealing with past pain is forgiveness. Forgiveness is not the same thing as reconciliation—it doesn't require anything of the other party. Nor does forgiving others minimize or erase any wrong done to you. It *does* release you from hanging on to the need to retaliate—to punish the offender. If you don't forgive, you stay connected to the pain. You remain a victim. And your roots are stunted.

Forgiveness doesn't always eliminate pain, but over time forgiveness *can* distance you from it. Only God is able to forgive once *and* forget. We forgive and remember and then have to forgive all over again. It's still worth the effort. Dealing with the pain of the past can enable you to embrace valuable parts of your heritage.

Here's what you can do. Make an effort to reconnect with distant or estranged family members. Ask family members to tell you stories. Research your ancestral roots. Doing these things can help build a rich heritage that can give you the anchor for growing new roots.

What If I Was Adopted?

If you were adopted you may have no contact with your biological family. Perhaps you haven't been interested in making contact. Or maybe you're someone who feels a real need to find those biological connections.

Some adoptees wrestle with questions about their heritage. Your brother may look just like Mom and your sister may have a temperament just like your grandfather, but you're compelled to ask, "Where does my blonde hair come from?" or "From whom did I get my sense of humor?" I'm not trying to create this need in your life. People who are adopted not only get a family, they get that family's root system, too. For many adoptees, grafting onto that root system is a smooth, unquestioned process. But for others—even those who have a fantastic experience with their adoptive families—there is a gnawing need to know more about biological beginnings. If you feel this need, know that it is valid and important. Wanting to answer these questions is not unloving or unappreciative toward the family who chose you and has loved you. Your questions are a natural result of wanting to become a rooted person.

If you choose to follow this path, you may have a variety of options for discovering your biological roots, depending on the circumstances of your adoption and the laws in your state. Start by having a conversation with your parents. You may be able to contact the adoption agency involved, and governmental agencies or courts may need to be involved depending on your situation and location. Don't fret if your situation or research doesn't bring you the results you desire. Remember that the roots you've been given by your adoptive parents are just as valid an anchor—and maybe more so—than those of your biological parents.

The Importance of Place

My wife's parents lived in the same house for twenty-five years. In this house the family of seven shared every aspect of their lives with one another. They took pride in the high quality of the family rendition of "Happy Birthday." This was the place where boyfriends (I was one) and girlfriends stopped by to meet the parents. The place where the deaths of grandparents and parents were mourned. And even the place where the children felt suddenly wealthy when the pool went in.

Christmas always framed the most and best memories for my wife's family. Everyone would gather on Christmas morning to open presents, beginning with the youngest. Children were always the most valued members of the gathering, and even now as adults they have fond memories of when they were the youngest and got to go first. Then there are the stories that get told over and over again. There was the year when Jennifer shouted "Leaping Lizards!" every time she opened a gift. And that year when all Robbie wanted was his "dings and sticks and things" (a drum set). We still like to look at the picture of him sitting behind the drums banging away. As the memories are recounted someone will invariably say, "Mamaw was with us that year" or "Did we still have the red carpet then?"

After twenty-five years in the same house my in-laws retired. They sold the house and moved to the country. When we're in the neighborhood—or anywhere nearby—our children ask if we can drive by the house just to remember. Not long ago my son asked if we could show his friend where his grandparents used to live. Other people live in the house now. But if they would ever want to sell it, we would combine our resources and buy it no matter how much it cost. It is a place of rich memories and deep roots.

Sacred spaces are important to us. And these "holy places" can be anywhere. At Christmastime, many people find a holy place in church—even people who don't traditionally attend church feel the pull of spiritual roots. My wife's "holy place" is the beach. She loves to feel the wind and the sun. She moves into a Zen-like state at the sound of the waves. She can lie on a beachside chair for hours. This kind of "worship" perplexes me. I get anxious at the constant moving of the waves. Why can't they be still for a few minutes? I prefer the mountains and woods and a lakeside cabin where I can embrace the quiet and breathe in the peace. I prefer a place where I can get up early and drink a cup of coffee by the water. In that holy place I feel wrapped in a womb, galaxies away from the problems of the world. I wish I were there now!

I spent my best childhood years in northeast Georgia. Our tiny town consisted of a post office, a café, two gas stations, and a small clothing assembly plant. It's probably representative of those good years that my brother moved back there after graduating from high school in Louisiana.

I have the most wonderful feeling when I go to visit him. Not just to see my brother, but because of that place. When we drive down the road that leads to this little town, peace and calm pour over my soul. We pass the small house our family lived in. I sometimes take a short detour to look at the elementary school and pause to remember playing football on the playground and jumping out of the swings.

I remember how people would gather in the evenings to just sit and talk at Seward's gas station. I remember buying a one-liter bottle of a soft drink and drinking it all, then filling it with water and drinking that too just to see if I could. This place connects me to my heritage—just being here helps me to extend some roots. I wonder if that is why my brother moved back there.

Maybe you need a place that helps you to connect, especially when life seems to come apart. After the destruction of the World Trade Center buildings on September 11, 2001, late-night TV host Conan O'Brien came back on the air on September 18. On that first show he told about just such a place:

I don't exactly know how we are going to do this. But
we're going to try to do it. . . . That's what a lot of people
here feel is the right thing to do — is get back and to try
our hardest to move forward and to make sense of our
lives at a time when absolutely nothing makes sense.
I don't talk about these things on air, but I was raised
Catholic. And today I did what I haven't done since
the first show when I went on the air. . . . So, I felt like
I needed someone or I needed something to help me. I
went across the street to St. Patrick's Cathedral and I sat
for a bit. And I'm glad I did. . . . Sitting there I felt this is
such a beautiful place.[2]

Recover What You Can

I need to talk a bit about another way to discover your heritage — but it's not as easy as digging up information on your history or reconnecting with a place. For some of you, it may bring back some of those bad memories. When I think about my relationship with my parents, I experience a variety of feelings. Certainly pain emanates from those memories. But remember what I said about forgiveness? Dealing with the pain through forgiveness, I can now see things I want to take into the future — experiences, traditions, and wisdom that I might otherwise have missed because of the pain.

From as early as I can remember (and probably even before), my mother read books to me. I have many memories of sitting in my mother's lap while she read to me. My mother gave me a love of reading. She took me to the library as a child, and during the summers I would check out and read dozens of books. I didn't know at the time how valuable this would be to my future. Today I sit at my computer *writing* a book.

I have tried intentionally to pass on the love of reading to my children. My wife and I read to them when they were small. As they've grown older, we've enjoyed taking them to the bookstore (and I have an "open wallet" policy when it comes to books). Yet it is only recently that I have recognized this part of my life as my mother's influence. I am grateful to her.

My mother provided something very important for my children. My eleven-year-old is working through *The Chronicles of Narnia* by C. S. Lewis. My fourteen-year-old discovered through his advanced placement English class that he reads and interprets literature quite well. He also seems to have some natural ability at writing. We talked about Edgar Allan Poe's short stories at home after he'd read them in school. And my sixteen-year-old has discussed *The Scarlet Letter* with us. She read it in her advanced placement English class. Interpretation and analysis of literature seems to come easily to her—she has no problem extricating Nathaniel Hawthorne's attitudes toward Puritanism.

Thanks, Mom.

My dad taught me about hard work. Though he died when I was thirteen, my memories of him are almost all set against the background of work. I can picture his shirt covered with white streaks left from drying perspiration during the season when he worked as a carpenter. His boots were sometimes completely soaked with sweat. When he worked on a ranch, I worked with him during the summers and discovered what it was like to leave early in the morning and return home at dark. We worked around the house, too. We worked in the garden. We mowed the grass. We built sheds. I wish I had memories of my dad playing ball with me or just having fun together—I grieve that I missed those things. But I also embrace what my dad did give me, a heritage of hard work.

A number of years ago I found an old aluminum lunch-box. It was scratched and banged up and the handle had been replaced. It was the lunchbox of a hardworking man. As soon as I saw it, I wanted it. It reminded me of my dad. He carried a similar lunchbox to work with him. My mom would pack it with his sandwiches and thermos, and at the end of the day he would bring it home empty. I keep this life-worn lunchbox on a shelf in my office. When I look at it I think of my dad and how hard he worked. I remember to bring my *own* lunch to work. And since I still struggle to believe that showing up to an office is actually "work," it reminds me to put on a blue-collar attitude in my white-collar job.

My parents also helped develop in me the belief that I could do anything if I just tried. My dad once told me that I should never say, "I can't do that." I was allowed to say, "I have never tried" or "I don't know how yet," but my dad never wanted me to say, "I can't." My mom told me that I could do or be anything I wanted. Even though my relationship with my mom has not been close for a long time, her words have survived the hurt and the distance. I can still hear her words just before I went off to first grade: "You can do anything if you try hard."

I believe that God has preserved my mother's words in my mind and heart to help me when I face uncertain circum-stances. I haven't appreciated everything in my heritage but some parts hold special value—they're worth holding on to and passing on.

You may have similar root-growing nuggets in your heritage. If they're embedded next to painful memories, grasping them may mean getting close to parts of your past that you probably have worked very hard to distance yourself from. Move slowly if you must. But go ahead. Take the risk. Be ready to apply plenty of forgiveness and you will discover roots that can deepen your life for the rest of your life.

Recover what you can.

Spiritual Heritage

Tumbleweeds are often drawn to spiritual things—but many don't have much of a personal spiritual history to draw from. Perhaps their parents gave up on religion or saw it as irrelevant and never introduced them to spirituality. But you may simply have to dig a little deeper to find a spiritual heritage. Ask questions. Listen to stories from your parents, grandparents, aunts, or uncles. The spiritual lives of those who came before you can give you another place to sink some roots.

I look back to my great-grandfather and find a place to connect some roots. I grew up knowing that my Pawpaw Wheat possessed a deep spiritual commitment. He served as a leader in his rural church. Pawpaw greatly impacted my dad's life and my dad told me how much he respected Pawpaw.

When I was eleven years old and living in Georgia, we received a phone call and learned that Pawpaw, who lived in Louisiana, had been diagnosed with terminal cancer. Immediately my dad telephoned Pawpaw. I stood beside my dad and looked up at him as he talked to Pawpaw on the phone. I only heard one side of the conversation, but I saw my dad cry for one of the few times in his life.

When he hung up the phone my dad told us what Pawpaw had said. He had asked Pawpaw if he was afraid. Pawpaw said, "No. No cancer is bigger than my God." Maybe to you that sounds sentimental or naive. But that one statement still shapes my life today. Pawpaw was not saying that he thought he wouldn't die. He was just saying that he possessed a spiritual reality more real than cancer. Or maybe Pawpaw would say that this spiritual reality possessed him. Someone related to me knew a spiritual life so real that it surpassed physical reality. I choose this as a place to plant my own spiritual life. I own this as my roots.

If you can't find a spiritual heritage in your family (and even if you can), you can still choose a spiritual heritage. History brims with examples that you may want to incorporate into your own life. I have chosen a tradition that values freedom while recognizing the importance of community and accountability. I look to Roger Williams as a hero of my heritage. Out of his own experiences of persecution, Roger Williams founded the colony that would become Rhode Island. Williams believed that England had no right to take land from the Native Americans, that people should practice faith in whatever way their conscience demanded or in no way if they chose, that the civil authorities had no authority in religious matters, and that women should be granted certain civil rights.[3] I'm glad to name Roger Williams as a part of my heritage.

I have a friend who finds security in the high structure of his spiritual heritage. I would find this heritage too confining. For me it is too defined and mandated. Yet he continues to see God working through the structures I would resist. He looks to different heroes than I do, and his heritage roots him in a place that is fertile soil.

Your spiritual heritage will likely be different from mine or my friend's. Seek it out. Or adopt one. Your roots will grab on to this heritage.

Hand Up the Story

As you discover your heritage—through family, place, spirituality, and more—and make connections to those roots, hand this story *up* to your children and grandchildren. When you have a heritage to share, you don't hand it *down*, you hand it *up*.

My experience tells me that receiving this story is of great value to your children and grandchildren. Recently, my father-in-law took my family back to the area where he grew up. He told stories of life as a child in central Texas. He showed us the house where Big Mama lived. He pointed to the places where his relatives had lived and showed us the places he played as a child. My children still talk about this trip. Someone will say, "How big was Big Mama?" (she weighed about 100 pounds) or "Tell me again about the cistern." My wife learned on this trip that her dad's middle name came from a creek bordering his parents' property. I know this isn't an earth-shattering discovery, but it did help her to sink some roots a little deeper.

As you hand your story up, your children and grandchildren will grow deeper roots. And they'll live a little taller.

Chapter Five

DEEPEN YOUR LIFE

*D*id you watch the NBC reality show *Average Joe*? On this show a beautiful young woman meets a group of average-looking guys and is charged with choosing a potential mate from this group. Or will she? Here comes the twist. A boatload of underwear-model type guys arrives to compete with the average guys. What will she decide? Could a beautiful young woman choose an average-looking man? Or will she choose someone on the basis of his appearance? Here's the real question: *Will this woman choose with her heart?*

This question distinguishes depth from shallowness. Making choices inconsistent with our heart is shallow living. Deep within our hearts is where we make connections to ourselves. Let's start searching deeply. Don't be afraid. You may be surprised at what you find. Roots will grow when you search your own heart deeply.

Using the mouth of Polonius in *Hamlet*, Shakespeare said, "To thine own self be true." Let's distinguish between being true to yourself and being selfish. Selfish people resemble a huge black hole. According to scientists, black holes are celestial objects with such dense mass that their gravitational pull draws everything into them. The theory states that the gravitational pull is so strong it even keeps light from shining out, hence the term black hole. You know people like this. So do I. One man talked to me about his wife's potential terminal illness. That wasn't so unusual, but his next statement shocked me. "But what I'm really concerned about is myself." Astonishing. Clearly a black hole sort of person. I quickly stepped away. I didn't want to fall in.

People true to themselves live so that life streams out of their hearts. The truest parts of you live in the deep. The kind of life I'm talking about looks more like a fountain than a black hole.

A fountain creates beauty as long as the water flows. The college I attended organized its campus around a quadrangle, in the center of which was a fountain. I think the fountain stayed in disrepair most of my college years. It was often dry. Of course, students contributed to the fountain's state, taking special delight in sabotaging it on days when dignitaries would be visiting the campus. Some days it was filled with soap. If not soap, catfish. These pranks probably seemed hilarious when they were conceived in some dorm room at 2 AM.

When the fountain failed to flow, it was useless. Without flow a fountain is a pool of stagnant water. People true to themselves flow. Life flows out of their hearts into every facet of living. Want to deepen the roots you already have growing? Ask yourself, "How's the flow? How's the flow from my heart to the rest of my life?" Does "who you are" pour out into every aspect of what you do, where you go, how you speak?

What would your life look like if you lived true to yourself? Some of us struggle to answer that question. We don't know exactly what's in our hearts. We've reacted. We've escaped. We've tried to fit in. But we haven't searched our hearts. If you've taken the step to begin to discover your heart, you're ahead of the game. If you haven't, why not get started now?

Discover Your Heart

Proverbs 4:23 states, "Above all else, guard your heart, for it is the wellspring of life." Guard it? I can't even find it! How can I figure out who I really am and connect to that person? I've lived my whole life trying to fit into others' expectations.

In *The Journey of Desire*, John Eldredge tells us that the key to our heart is our desire. Most of us have discovered our surface desires. We love chocolate or sports cars or, in my case, turkey and dressing at Thanksgiving. These surface desires aren't necessarily bad. But they shouldn't define our lives. Living on the surface, these desires can't help us grow deep roots. To grow roots, we'll need to search out our *heart's* desire.

I want to introduce you to a certain story of Jesus that amazes me. The gospel of Luke tells the story. As Jesus and His followers left the city of Jericho they passed a blind man. Jews often traveled through Jericho to Jerusalem for religious festivals, so seeing a blind man sitting along the road wouldn't have been notable—it was the perfect place for people who were dependent on the charity of others to look for handouts. Surely people heading to a religious festival would be charitable.

The gospel of Mark tells us that this particular blind man was called Bartimaeus. Bartimaeus means "Son of Timaeus," or, for us, "Son of Timothy." Did they give him a name? Or did they just call him Timothy's boy? Bartimaeus was like thousands of others in the ancient world who moved through life without a name or voice. Even in this story, Bartimaeus at first faded into the background. Jesus and His followers walked past him without noticing at all. But somehow, Bartimaeus noticed

Jesus and started yelling. He wouldn't stop yelling for Jesus. Jesus couldn't help but notice Bartimaeus, and called for this insistent blind man.

Here's where we get to the crazy part of the story. Look at Jesus' response to Bartimaeus. Jesus asked, "What do you want me to do for you?" What an amazing question. Though it may have seemed obvious what Bartimaeus would have wanted, Jesus didn't simply restore his sight. And He didn't ask this question flippantly. He invited Bartimaeus to speak from his heart's desire. *What do you want?*

In this story, we get to see God as someone who cares what we want. Perhaps you've thought of God as someone who may deal occasionally with the world's problems but is not so interested in your own. Many people think of God as an angry tyrant. I've had someone tell me they went to a church that believed in a God who was distant until He noticed someone having fun. Then this version of God showed up just in time to stop the fun. This same aberration of God would be waiting for you to want something so He could make sure you'd never get it. With many of these pictures of God, we learn that we shouldn't have any desires—that we should have no wants. Desires have been painted as antispiritual. John Eldredge says that God draws us out by our desires. Isn't that what Jesus did with Bartimaeus?

The question Jesus asked Bartimaeus could be the same question you need to consider in order to discover your heart. *What do you want?* Not, "What is expected?" Not, "What is my reaction?" Not, "What am I afraid of?" *What do I want?* What do I truly want? At the deepest level, what is the life I want to live? Bartimaeus answered immediately. He had probably been meditating on that very question for years. But our immediate answers may not reveal our real hearts. If we answer out of habit we may answer out of our surface desires instead of our heart's desire. Our quick answers might be, "I want to win the lottery" or "I want to be twenty-five again."

Bartimaeus told Jesus that he wanted to see. Think of what it would have meant for Bartimaeus to see. Of course, he would experience the wonderful sights and colors and lights that he had missed out on for so many years. But more than an ability to recognize beauty, Bartimaeus would suddenly have gained social significance and standing. What would you say was in Bartimaeus' heart? He wanted more than anything to live as a participating member of his community. He wanted to have the ability to care for himself. Can you see him praying every day for some kind of miracle? The miracle he prayed for was much more than the physical capacity to see.

What does your heart desire at the deepest level? A friend of mine recently built a large new home. You might think, "Yea, that's it. A big new house, that's what I *really* want!" For my friend, it wasn't the house that meant so much. If you ask him about the house he'll first tell you about his gratitude. Then he'll tell you *why* he is so grateful for the house. This past Thanksgiving his entire family gathered for the long holiday weekend. Five children, their spouses, ten grandchildren, a brother-in-law, a sister-in-law, mother-in-law, father-in-law, two nephews, a niece, and other guests showed up to celebrate together. There were between twenty-five and thirty people in his house. And they all fit. He wanted a place where the family could gather together. What does he really want? He wants a place to build family relationships. He wants his family to stay close. The big house is just one way to get there.

What do you really want—what is your heart's desire? You may find your heart better if you write down some things. Put on paper what it is that seems to be at the center of what you want. No need to be in a hurry. Your objective is to grow roots, not race through this exercise (or this book). Go ahead and take time now. Write down what you think may be your heart's desire. After you write these things down, you can come back to them in a few days and reevaluate what you wrote.

If it helps, think of yourself as Bartimaeus. Close your eyes and put yourself in the story. (Wait, don't close your eyes just yet. Read a little bit further first.) Here you sit with your life dominated by surface desires. Isn't that Jesus coming down the road? He comes right by you, stops, and calls you by name. He knows your name. Then He asks you, "What do you want Me to do for you?" You can tell by the look in His eyes and the sincerity of His voice that He really wants to know. But how will you answer? How would you answer if you believed that Jesus really wanted to know and could make your heart's desires come true? Take your time; He's not in a hurry. (Okay, now you can close your eyes for a moment. Try this. Then come back to the book when you're ready.)

If this exercise is difficult for you, it may be because you have a barrier that keeps you from hearing the sincerity of Jesus' question and responding with equal honesty. The barrier that made this question difficult for me was shame. Shame settled on my life like a fog back when I was in the second grade and it didn't lift for a long time. There I was in a new school again. I had begun attending class right as they were preparing to present a school program. Even though I was new, the teacher said I could have a part in the program if I would promise to participate. Just being in the program helped me to feel more connected to this school and these people. During school on program day the teacher reminded us that "this was the night!" We practiced to get everything just right. The teacher emphasized how important it was for us to be on time. I was really looking forward to this shared experience.

When I told my mom about the program, she said I couldn't go. She worked nights as a waitress at a bar and couldn't get away. I asked her to arrange for someone else to take me and told her how important it was, that they were counting on me. She refused. She and her live-in boyfriend dropped me off at the babysitter's. I asked why he couldn't give me a ride to the program. She just said, "No."

I sat at the babysitter's house lonely, sad, and ashamed. I felt ashamed that I couldn't take care of my responsibility. I felt ashamed that my mom worked in a bar. I felt ashamed that my mom had a live-in boyfriend. And if the things my mom said about my dad were true, I felt doubly ashamed about that, too. I was ashamed of my parents and my living condition and I was ashamed of myself. I guess when you're eight years old you can't tell the difference between being ashamed of your parents and being ashamed of yourself.

Shame hides in the background of everything that's happened in my life. Why couldn't I open up and let people in? Why couldn't I have a sense of pride about my accomplishments? I was ashamed of myself. Then one day . . . that changed. On a Monday morning as I was practicing some of the disciplines I talk about in another chapter, I thought about the school program incident. I felt the shame. I felt sad and unimportant. And I realized that those feelings which crept into my life then had stayed with me. I had owned a shame that was not mine.

I describe what happened next as looking over the top of dark glasses. It felt as if I had been wearing a pair of dark glasses all of my life. I put these glasses on when I was eight but forgot to take them off. I lived through those dark lenses all my life without knowing they were there. On that Monday morning I pulled the glasses down on my nose and looked over them for the first time in more than thirty years. You know what?

The world is a beautiful place when you aren't seeing it through your shame.

I didn't just see things anew. I *heard* something in a way I had never heard it before. *What do you want?* I heard it in a new way because now I wasn't ashamed to look for the answer. It had taken a while, but grace finally overcame shame. It may take a while for you to be able to answer this question, too. Even if you currently live in the fog, keep searching for your heart's answer. When you're able, look over the top of your dark sunglasses. Trust my experience. Don't give up.

Nurture Your Heart

When you begin to discover your heart you will also want to nurture it. Remember Proverbs 4:23: "Above all else, guard your heart, for it is the wellspring of life." Guarding your heart doesn't mean putting a wall around it. Some of us struggle because we've walled off our heart from the rest of our lives. The pain we experienced makes us want to protect ourselves. When we separate our everyday life from our heart, we compartmentalize. And life becomes shallow.

Roots inch deeper when you integrate your heart into the rest of your life. Connect your heart to your values. Make decisions that value the desires of your heart. If you don't intentionally decide to value the desires of your heart, you'll probably default to the predominant values around you. These predominant values—things like rampant consumerism—can suffocate your heart.

Rampant consumerism has already cut off much of our air supply. If we could somehow escape this consumerism we would breathe anew. We consumers cave far too easily to the pressure of advertisers, allowing them to create discontent in our lives. We're told we will be happy if we possess this thing that is "more," "new," or "improved." Consumerism attracts tumbleweeds. Don't be naive. This is a fatal attraction: As we become better consumers we damage our hearts.

Have you ever wondered why gluttony is one of the seven deadly sins? (Besides after a particularly "successful" visit to the local buffet restaurant, that is.) What is so bad about eating more than you need? The problems with gluttony become clear when we broaden gluttony to include more than eating. Let's include overconsumption of all kinds. What happens when we continue to consume more and more of what we don't really need? Our closets and garages become the overstuffed boneyards of our consumption. And our heart's true desire gets hidden by the clutter of our never-ending desire for more stuff. When do we ever have enough? You could use a new/bigger/better car, house, TV . . . right?

Oh, but to get that new/bigger/better car, house, or TV you'll have to work longer hours or move to a different job. This consumerism damages our families and other relationships. It can even redefine our relationships (and not in a good way) because to get more we have to climb on top of others. We have no qualms about using them as stepstools because we want to—we *need* to—move ahead. Listen, this is a deadly sin. It's deadly to others as we disregard them or abuse them so we can consume more. It's deadly to our hearts. Our gluttony has made "heart disease" an epidemic.

This consumerism is just one way we disconnect our hearts from our lifestyles. You may think of a myriad of ways that your heart remains disconnected from your everyday life. The question you must answer is, *How can I run streams from the wellspring of my heart to the rest of my life?* It wouldn't hurt to make a list of practical things you can do that might reflect the wellspring. Let me help you get started. Here are a few possibilities:

- Take cookies to your neighbor or rake their leaves or serve them in another way.
- Get in touch with a friend or family member you haven't talked to in a long time.
- Spend an evening with your family but leave the TV off.
- Take a walk in the park, in the woods, or at the beach. Spend some time with yourself.
- Create something—draw, paint, or do something to express your creativity.
- Journal every day for a week. Allow your heart to speak on the page.

Choose something on your list and do it. Then come back to your list in a few days or weeks and choose something else to try. Practice the things that reflect who you are at the deepest level. And if it overwhelms you to make a list, just think of *one* thing and begin it.

Decorate Your Life

My friend Ann has a beautifully decorated house. You would enjoy being at her home—especially relaxing in her warm, comfortable den. Something about the furnishings just fits together, but the real beauty lives in more than just the pieces of furniture and art. The real beauty lives in the stories behind the objects in the room. Ann guarantees the long life of these decorations by regularly recounting the stories to her young-adult daughters. She knows that one day she and her husband will be gone and that her daughters (and one day to come, grandchildren) can experience deep rootedness from the stories that decorate her house. When you walk into Ann's home you see the artifacts of a life. These decorations didn't originate in a department store or factory; they came from her heart.

Ever heard of feng shui? I don't know much about it, and I

may not agree with it theologically, but the growing popularity of this decorating philosophy suggests that lots of people are deciding the space they live in *matters*. Feng shui proposes that there is a definite "right place" for things—that the arrangement of furniture impacts the "feel" of a given room. Many people are moving away from "decorating to impress" and, instead, trying to create a living space that connects them to a deep place—to a spiritual place. Perhaps they're drawn to this philosophy because they really want to live in a place that is more connected to their hearts.

How would your living space change if it were connected to your heart? Look at how the space is organized today. Many of us organize our primary living space around the TV. Is that what we really want? What would your living space look like if it were organized around the landscape of your heart?

I recently discovered a gift for my daughter's graduation. I wanted to give her something that would connect with her heart; something that would help her to grow deep roots. An artifact of life—not unlike the memories that fill Ann's den. Want to know what I found? I just discovered that I could buy an ancient pilgrim's badge. You may not be familiar with these. In medieval times a pilgrim would travel to important sacred sites as a spiritual pilgrimage. While at these sites, they would buy a badge to commemorate the trip. I think this is a great gift for my daughter's high school graduation.

The pilgrim's badge would remind my daughter of the journey she has made thus far and encourage her to continue the pilgrimage. I'll probably give her other things as well, like a new computer and stuff for her dorm room. But I don't want to simply be utilitarian or help her stay on top of the latest trends. I want to give her something that will connect her life to her heart. She'll need these roots over the next few years while she discovers more of what her life's about in the context of a larger world. I hope she chooses to fill her material world with things that come from the heart. I long for my daughter's entire life to take the shape of her heart.

Take the Necessary Time

I'll just say it right up front: Deepening your life is time-consuming. It's a slow process. Some of us nod or wave at the importance of a deeper life but never get around to taking it seriously. We *intend* to. We look forward to that "one day soon" when life will slow down enough for us to be intentional about connecting our hearts and lives. Then we rush out of the house late for work. Or we rush home to prepare dinner so we can collapse and dread another day.

While riding on this merry-go-round at a dizzying pace, two things jolted me. The first was a simple scene that captured my attention after visiting a friend in the hospital. As I was leaving the hospital, hurrying off to some relatively unimportant activity, I was forced to sidestep a four- or five-year-old girl who had stopped on the sidewalk. She had crouched to touch a pansy that was planted near the sidewalk. The girl's mother stood about ten feet ahead of her on the sidewalk. She looked back, her face showing impatience, and repeated several times, "Come on. Hurry up!"

I had already walked past the scene when suddenly I stopped dead in my tracks. I turned and watched. The little girl was exploring and experiencing the wonder of life. The simple beauty of a pansy had captured her. She wouldn't linger there for very long—in a few moments she would move on to another wonder or beauty. But the mom couldn't wait. Now, I don't want to be too hard on the mom. I have no idea what was happening in her life. She was leaving the hospital and may have been experiencing a great deal of stress. The mom was not abusive, just in a hurry.

But the mom was not my concern. What stunned and paralyzed me was that I saw myself in this scene. As I had hurriedly and impatiently stepped around this little girl I realized this was *my* story, and in the voice of this mother I could hear myself saying, "Come on. Hurry up!" I wondered if the words I most often used with my children were *hurry up*?

I felt another powerful jolt while reading the book *The Life You've Always Wanted* by John Ortberg. The book contains a chapter entitled *The Unhurried Life*. Through this funny and insightful chapter I diagnosed myself with "hurry sickness." Ortberg listed some of the symptoms of hurry sickness as "constantly speeding up daily activities, multiple-tasking, and clutter." (Obviously, I mention these so you can make a self-diagnosis.)

Ortberg says that people with hurry sickness hate waiting. As we approach a stoplight with two or more lanes, we count the number of cars in each lane. Then we choose the lane with the fewest number of cars. We make the same kind of calculations at grocery store checkout lanes. And if the hurry sickness has become acute, we watch the person "who would have been me" in the other line as we inch forward. If we finish our purchase before they do, we win! If they finish first, we berate ourselves for a bad choice. This sickness has so infected our culture that "we invented the Drive-Thru Lane to enable families to eat in vans, as nature intended."[1]

Ortberg also mentions multiple-tasking and clutter as symptoms of hurry sickness. Do you need to be constantly engaged in multiple activities at once? What other things are you doing while reading this book? Eating, watching TV, listening to music, talking on the phone? And about that clutter thing—look around. What do you see? Don't forget the invisible clutter (the half-done projects, missed appointments, and all that stuff you forgot).

Okay, so we're too busy. What does this have to do with growing roots, connecting with our hearts, and deepening our lives? Ortberg says that the by-product of hurry sickness is "superficiality." Relationships are superficial because we hurry through them so fast that real love never develops. We arrive at home at the end of the day too fatigued to connect. Then we attempt to escape the hurry and fatigue by participating in activities that lead to further superficiality or even destruction. We "veg out" in front of the TV, mindlessly surf on the Internet, or turn to alcohol to numb us.

We continue living shallow lives when we try to address heart issues with quick fixes. I think this may explain the popularity of TV shows like *Extreme Makeover*. Along with our proclivity for voyeurism, we like to think that if we could address our surface appearance, our lives would change. "My life would be whole if I could just look different!" But maybe we should listen to Dr. Phil: "Nose jobs, breast implants, liposuction, Botox . . . you name it people are doing it. In 2002, 6.6 million people had cosmetic surgery. But what if changing your outside doesn't fix your inside?"[2]

Extreme Makeover ends when the made-over person returns home to an unveiling. There's even a term for this unveiling: "the reveal." The reveal is often dramatic, including excitement, tears, and astonishment. But what may be more "revealing" is whatever happens next—the part we don't see on television. What happens the next day, next week, next month, next year to someone who has changed their outward appearance, but not necessarily their inside? Liposuction can't fix a sick, broken heart.

Supermodel Janice Dickinson appeared on the Dr. Phil show. "I've been on the cover of every magazine in the world," she said. "But as a young model, I never felt as beautiful as I looked. I masked it well with alcoholism. I grew up in an abusive home and was told on a daily basis by my father that I would never amount to anything and that I looked like a boy. One of the main reasons I got a lot of plastic surgery was because of the voice of my father. I've had my boobs and eyes done, my forehead lifted, and my stomach done. Every six months I fly to Dallas to get Botox and I also get collagen injections. I'm addicted to cosmetic surgery! But plastic surgery hasn't stifled the voice of my father. Dr. Phil, how do I make this go away?"[3]

Did you see the painful truth in her words? "Plastic surgery hasn't stifled the voice of my father." Some people try to fix heart issues with plastic surgery. Others use money, an accumulation of possessions, power, or status. Yet none of these can open your life to the streams flowing from your heart. Slow down; take some time to rediscover your heart. Then allow your *heart* to determine the course of your life.

Chapter Six

FIND A COMMUNITY

I've already talked about the importance of discovering your heritage. Another source of identity comes from the people we *currently* share life with. We discover who we are in a web of relationships.

I remember being five or six years old and seeing TV ads for the upcoming Sunday night movie, *The Wizard of Oz*. Conflicted emotions overcame my small psyche. I wanted so much to see Dorothy and Toto on the yellow brick road. But every time I thought of Dorothy and Toto, I couldn't help but see frightening images in my mind. I couldn't escape the mental pictures of that wicked witch and those flying monkeys. By the time Sunday rolled around I couldn't bring myself to watch the movie.

When I got older, the witches and monkeys didn't scare me so much, and I finally saw the entire movie. Now I could stop obsessing with what frightened me and identify with Dorothy's traveling companions. I too felt like a part of me was still to be discovered and lived out. I hoped it wasn't just a dream. I didn't want to wake up to find that I was hopelessly stuck as less than a whole person.

It wasn't until much later that I realized that I could grow into a whole self through the same process used by the lion, the tin man, and the scarecrow. I could journey with a group of trusted companions. Somehow walking with others grows me into the whole person I was meant to be. Knowing who we are in our web of relationships can make the difference when the flying monkeys attack and life looks like it may come apart.

Have you ever felt life nearly pull you apart? Mark and Julie had struggled to get pregnant. At first they enjoyed the frequency of the "conception attempts" (bet you've never heard it called *that* before). But after a while, that to-be-enjoyed-in-marriage activity became so pressure-filled that it seemed like a duty. Then there was the medical testing which left them feeling like lab rats. Finally, with persistence and medical intervention, Julie became pregnant. Mark and Julie excitedly reported the pregnancy to families and friends who had been supporting them through the process. They all celebrated the event.

A few weeks after their announcement, Julie began to experience problems with the pregnancy. Mark and Julie's families and friends transitioned from celebrating to praying and worrying with them. Sadly, as you've probably guessed by now, Julie miscarried. After such effort and anticipation, hopes were dashed. Celebrations were replaced with grieving.

How do you find help to deal with this kind of pain? Mark and Julie struggled through the kind of grief you probably know about. The miracle in their life came not because they were spared the pain but because a group of friends walked with them through it. When you share joy, it multiplies. When you share grief, it divides. It doesn't hurt any less, but it does become manageable.

The kind of violent storms we encounter in life — like the one Mark and Julie faced — can disrupt or pull apart relationships. Yet even the "perfect storm" will be hard-pressed to damage lives that are tightly knitted into community — into a web of life-giving relationships.

Allow me to talk about trees for a moment. (Hang in there, this will all make perfect sense.) Redwoods are truly amazing trees. Many people who frequent redwood forests talk about the spiritual atmosphere that permeates the self-renewing grove of ancient trees. Standing in a redwood circle feels like standing in a cathedral.

Redwoods have been growing on this planet for 160 million years. Many individual redwood trees are between 600 and 1,200 years old. Some have lived for 2,000 years. Redwood trees are resistant to fire and even *need* fire to survive. Their wood is not susceptible to rot from water and they repel insects that may cause damage.

The redwood root system plays an important role in their longevity. Unlike other conifers, redwoods don't have a taproot. Instead redwoods grow a network of shallow roots that extend for hundreds of feet. Since redwoods grow in groves, the roots of one redwood entangle with the roots of another. Each giant tree is held in place by the root system of several other trees. This network of roots supports tree growth for hundreds and thousands of years to such an impressive stature.[1]

People, like redwoods, can never grow to great heights alone. They need a system of support. And while the deep roots we can grow alone are important, when we grow a network of horizontal roots — a web of life-giving relationships — we can stand against almost any destructive force. Remember these wise words:

By yourself you're unprotected.
With a friend you can face the worst.
Can you round up a third?
A three-stranded rope isn't easily snapped.
(Ecclesiastes 4:12, MSG)

Establishing and keeping this web of relationships we call community doesn't happen as easily as it once did. I have a friend named Mary who is in her seventies. I've talked with her several times about the events surrounding her husband's terminal illness, eventual death, and funeral service. She has mentioned more than once how much her friends, her church, and her neighbors gave to her while she was going through the grieving process. Mary also told me that things aren't quite the way they used to be. Mary wasn't just reminiscing about the *good old days.* I think she has noticed a qualitative difference in the way people live.

Mary has lived in the same small town of about 1,200 people for most of her life. She's lived in her current house for almost forty years. When she moved into this house, she became next-door neighbors to her best friend, Sweetie. Not long after the move, another best friend, Thelma, moved into the house across the street. Nearly every evening for more than thirty years, Mary and Sweetie would sit in a swing in Sweetie's front yard. Thelma usually walked across the street to join them. Before dark the entire neighborhood would drive by. Many stopped to chat through a car window. Others got out of their cars to sit and talk for a while. Mary, Sweetie, and Thelma stayed connected to one another and to the rest of the neighborhood.

A few years ago Sweetie died. A year and a half ago Thelma died. Over the years, new residents who don't know about the evening ritual have replaced many of the neighborhood regulars. No one stops to talk anymore. Remarkably, Mary still finds ways to share community. She gathers on Wednesday afternoons with a group of friends to prepare a meal for her church. The other day I waved at Mary as she sat on the porch with three new friends from her neighborhood. Mary understands that community, while it may be more difficult to achieve today, is still worth the effort.

A web of life-giving relationships is more than a luxury; it is a necessity for those who want to find a sense of meaning in life. Edward Hallowell, a psychiatrist, recounts his own need for a web of life-giving relationships in his book *Connect*. Hallowell tells about the importance of the friends he plays squash with:

> I remember a fellow resident of mine being shocked one day when he heard me say to a senior attending who had just offered me a job, "Will the position allow me to leave early on Tuesdays so I can play squash?"
>
> "How could you have asked that?" my friend gasped later. "Don't you know how hard it is to get that job?"
>
> But there is always a job. There isn't always a friend, however.

Hallowell goes on to say, *It is, in its own way, as important as church.*

Several factors contribute to the formation of these life-giving relationships. The participants have made these relationships a priority. They don't leave it to chance. They keep a regular routine—the squash game is followed by a cup of coffee or a beer and always conversation. Some of these relationships have been growing for twenty years. Hallowell also says, "Over time, the magic happens."[2]

Prioritize for Community

Especially in these times of cultural windstorms, the search for and maintenance of community ought to demand a high priority in our lives. Perhaps in the past—back when people like Mary and Sweetie and Thelma shared daily front-porch chats—community happened naturally or without much effort. Or maybe we simply used to value building relationships more highly. Whatever the case, it now takes a conscious effort to put life-giving relationships at the top of our priority lists. Our culture does not naturally move us to connect with one another.

We're an impatient people in an impatient world. We too quickly throw away relationships before they ever have a chance to take root. Though we instinctively desire the kinds of relationships Hallowell describes, we don't make lifestyle choices that allow these relationships to develop. For community to work, people have to agree together that this web of relationships is an important component in their daily lives.

Why would anyone *not* want community? Some of us have spent so much time living alone that we dismiss the importance of community. We've grown accustomed to a disconnected life. It's the "new normal." Maybe we never imagined that we could connect to another person in a meaningful and personal way. Maybe we've resigned ourselves to life without community. This may not be what we really want but it's like a hot, dry Texas summer—we just can't do anything about it.

Then there are those of us who have been hurt badly by others. (If this still stings when you read it, maybe it's time to revisit chapter 4, where I explore the value of forgiveness.) People we loved and trusted wounded us and were insensitive to our vulnerability. Our scars and calluses scream warnings that real community is not advisable in these dangerous days.

But just when we're ready to give up on meaningful relationships, a yearning to connect overcomes us. We find ever so small pockets of hope—hope that signals the possibility that we really could connect with a life-giving web of relationships.

Develop a Routine

Life must develop a certain amount of consistency for roots to grow. Want to test this theory? Don't water one of your plants regularly. Just water it . . . oh . . . whenever. Move it around once in a while. Assuming the plant is still alive after a few weeks, compare the roots with a similar plant that enjoyed consistent watering. I think you know what you'd discover.

Hallowell tells about a group of women who built routines to nurture their sense of community. Maeve, one of these women, describes the routines and rituals as:

Simple things. We go to eat, then we all sit together in a room. Sometimes we light candles and have a ceremony if one of us is moving in or out of a career. We have some spiritual rituals, too. For example, if somebody is going through a hard time, we spend a while just letting them speak, unconditionally supporting them and talking.[3]

If you're noticing that community has an inherent spiritual nature, you're zeroing in on a key concept. Let's zoom in closer. Maeve says:

We feel a sense of being for each other, not just doing activities together. . . . We trust in the unseen things in the world—because we've known each other, and gone through our lives together, and made it possible for us to say, "Well, I can trust in the unknown in my life, in what I can't see, because I know you're doing that with me. I

share that with you and that allows me to do more." . . .
Miraculous things seem to happen.[4]

Trust in the unseen. Does that sound familiar? We've circled back to a spiritual truth. I believe God is community. It just makes sense to me. I have come to a Trinitarian understanding of God where I experience God as Father, Son, and Spirit. And if my experience is true, it suggests we're wired for community. Maybe that's why Hallowell says his web of relationships is "as important as church." Perhaps the spiritual component in community is both an echo and a taste of the divine community that God draws us into.

It's probably no surprise then that many people search for community through a religious or spiritual organization. Spiritual curiosity is at an all-time high in a world marked by uncertainty. Not every religious group or church, however, is a life-*giving* web of relationships. Some of these organizations are life-*sapping*.

But don't use that reality as an excuse for not seeking a life-giving church. You may have given up on church as a means for finding community. You may be tempted to skip this section where I will encourage you not to give up. I don't blame you. A life-sapping church can do much damage. But I hope you will read on. I believe that these groups can be helpful and may be indispensable. I, for one, *need* a spiritual community—a place where I can honestly explore mystery, doubt, faith, and beauty. I yearn to share these things among a group of people who will also share their lives with me. Participating in a church can give us a framework for these webs of relationship. It can provide us with structure, routine, and ritual.

Groups that provide real opportunities to grow in community—real opportunities to live out who God wired us to be—are invaluable. You may have to look a little harder, a little longer, and a little further than you might expect to find one that's right for you. A traditional church with choirs, pews, and a steeple-topped building may look the part—and *may* be just right for you—or you may need to consider other options, like the one Stacey fell into when she wasn't looking.

Stacey left home right after high school, anxious to leave the dysfunction in her home. She distanced herself from her parents as soon as possible. In the distance, Stacey also lost her way, choosing a lifestyle marked by destructive behavior and relationships.

Feeling alone and directionless, Stacey wandered into a meeting of an "alternative" church. Nothing about this group reminded her of anything she'd previously known of church (and that was a good thing). The atmosphere of acceptance seemed almost tangible. Stacey doesn't remember what the leaders said during the meeting or anything about the message. She does remember that several people immediately offered her friendship. Though still defensive and wary, she decided to give this group a try.

Over a period of time, Stacey has made true friendships, found a job that meets her income needs, discovered people who support her attempts to make healthy life choices, and taken significant steps in her spiritual journey. The people she found in this spiritual community grew into the web of life-giving relationships she needed. When she had to change apartments, several people helped her move. When Stacey struggles with questions about life and spirituality, others listen. They sometimes share their own experiences. Mostly, they just spend time together. They are good friends.

Stacey doesn't attribute the changes in her life to any special church program, teaching, or a fancy building. Nor does she feel pressured to adopt a particular worldview. Stacey discovered community because she discovered acceptance and support. And she is growing deep roots.

I admit that acceptance, friendship, and support are not always the first things you find in a church. But many leaders are rediscovering the value and meaning of community and are working to transform their church into a true and accepting congregation. If you are able to find this kind of church, plant yourself there. A growing, healthy spiritual connection can give you the routine and help you develop the rituals to grow deep roots of community.

Give It Time

Do you detect a recurring theme in this book? Yes, community requires time to grow. There is no such thing as "instant" community. Instant acceptance (like Stacey's experience), sure. But community is best simmered in a slow cooker rather than zapped in a microwave.

Dr. Hallowell has participated in his web of relationships for twenty years. Maeve has been working on her friendships for over twenty years. Mary sits on the porch with friends she's known for fifty years. I wonder if I have a web of relationships that will last twenty or fifty years. The longer I hang in there with people who are life-giving, the more I can grow roots.

But there's one more obstacle to building community. Only recently have I noticed this tendency in my life: I sometimes view relationships as disposable.

The CD-ROM drive on our computer at home crashed so I checked into getting it fixed. Though the computer is ancient in computer years, it is still serviceable, except for the broken CD drive. I thought I would fix it and avoid spending the money for a new machine. My wife asked a technology expert at work about getting the CD-ROM drive repaired. He told her it wouldn't be worth the money. "You might as well buy a new machine," he said. Who would have thought that computers were disposable products? If yours breaks down, just trash it and get a new one.

While I may have been behind the times in my understanding of computer obsolescence, I was certainly "ahead of my time" when it came to how I treated some of my relationships. In the past, when something went wrong I would simply toss the relationship and look for a new one. I'm smarter now. I "get it" that as computers grow old they become obsolete. I've also learned that as relationships age they grow in value. In the world of computers, the latest model will probably serve you best. But for community, the earlier the vintage the more valuable the web of relationships become for growing roots.

I just watched another season of the TV reality show *Survivor.* Okay, you caught me. I wasn't watching the show for research or to better understand our shallow culture. I *like* the show. The concept intrigues me. These people spend forty days with one another removed from the distractions of our media- and technology-saturated world. They share life collectively for weeks, doing everything together. They share victory as teams, overcome challenges, and survive with the help of one another. This seems like fertile ground to grow the roots of community.

Yet on the reflection show for this particular season, Rob, one of the final three survivors, said that he never really became friends with anyone. He said he was constantly strategizing and repositioning himself. Rob showed the signs of friendship if it advanced him. He became an ally if it served his purpose. Where others thought he was showing allegiance, Rob was actually competing. He admitted that he played the game well because he always asked the question, "Where do I stand in comparison with everyone else?"

Rob's intention on *Survivor* was to win. As I listened to Rob I was forced to ask myself a question: What is my intention in life? Am I just trying to win? Am I constantly comparing where I stand on the status ladder to where neighbors and friends stand? Do I think of my work as a *competition* against my colleagues? At church, do I hide behind carefully constructed walls so people don't get to know the real me? The imperfect, flawed me?

I believe with all of my heart that the only way to *win* is to be rooted in community. Any definition of winning that does not include a web of life-giving relationships is false. I admit I struggle to put this heartfelt belief into practice. Perhaps you do, too. We may need to change the lens through which we view relationships. Maybe when we meet people we ought to see them not as the competition but as a possible strand of this web, people we could share life with. People who can help us experience the community God wired us for.

Chapter Seven

DEVELOP DISCIPLINES

*T*he Robbie Seay Band plays a song called "Faith of Our Fathers." One line of the song says, "*We are not alone . . . we did not begin here.*" I love that. It reminds me that my life is anchored to something ancient—something bigger than myself. A faith that began a long time ago shapes my life today. Another line of the song says, "*And to all who've gone before we are crying thank you.*" Other people planted seeds that now grow in my life. I live out of roots that began growing centuries ago. My ancient community of faith has handed me important practices that help me sink my roots deeper and deeper. *Thank you.*

"Faith of Our Fathers" puts in poetic form what I feel when I practice some of the spiritual disciplines. This kind of connection reminds me of imagery in Hebrews 11 (the faith chapter). Hebrews 11 recaps stories of faithful women and men who followed God. It tells of Noah who somehow heard . . . and chose to obey God's radical command to build a boat. It describes Abraham's decision to willingly leave his homeland and wander in search of God's promise. It tells about Moses and Isaac and Jacob and Joseph. And more. And then, after reminding us of these people who demonstrated great faith—who followed God even though they didn't know where He was leading them—we discover that these very heroes of the faith are *cheering us on.*[1]

The author paints a picture of a great arena. The stands are full. People are shouting and waving their arms in the air. One guy thrusts a big foam "We're number one" finger to the sky. I look at that foam finger. I study it closely. It has my name printed on it. Wait a minute. They're cheering for me! Do you see a foam finger with your name on it?

I'm standing on the field ready to run the race of a lifetime and the crowd is cheering me on. This scene resembles the climax to the movie *Rudy*. Rudy had wanted all his life to play football for his father's favorite football team, Notre Dame. On Saturday afternoons every autumn into winter, they'd sit mesmerized, staring at the TV, absorbed by the game. Everyone knew Rudy was too small and too slow to play football for Notre Dame. He wasn't even smart enough to get admitted as a student—at least not right out of high school.

After two years at another school, Rudy is accepted into Notre Dame. He tries out for the football team as a non-scholarship walk-on player. Miraculously, Rudy makes the practice squad, not because of his talent but because of his hard work. He spends two years practicing with the players, working as a member of the scout team. While "scout team" may sound glamorous, it's not. He and the other members of this practice squad would take the field in the positions of players they'd be facing in the next game, after which they were summarily pounded by the starting offense.

Rudy didn't dress out for a game. He never even saw the sidelines on game day, much less the playing field . . . until the very last game in Rudy's final year at Notre Dame, when his fellow team members convinced the coach to allow Rudy to don his uniform and join them. Standing on the sideline for the entire game, Rudy wants desperately to get into the game. With only a few seconds left in the game, the team and crowd start chanting, "Rudy, Rudy, Rudy." Reluctantly, the coach sends Rudy into the game. And as he stands on the field for the first time, the fans are cheering. This time they're cheering for Rudy.

When I practice certain spiritual disciplines I feel like Rudy. I can hear those ancient voices cheering for me. I can see that foam finger with my name on it. I feel a connection to those who practiced faith before me—I'm not in this alone.

My roots grow all the way back to the ancients mentioned in Scripture. I also sink roots into the experience of other pilgrims. Early monks passed to me *The Jesus Prayer.* St. Augustine reminds me to confess. St. John of the Cross teaches me about living through darkness. C. S. Lewis tells stories of mythic proportion and shines light into my life. Brennan Manning opens for me a life of grace.

Those who have gone before me light the path for this race. They teach me that this race isn't about winning—it's about finishing. They remind me that I can grow spiritual roots as long as I don't give up. As long as I stay in the race I can keep moving forward.

I want to tell you about the spirituality I have chosen to embrace. I have chosen differently from many of the world's spiritual seekers. Countless seekers have opted for an eclectic spirituality—a cafeteria-style faith. Imagine walking through a cafeteria of spiritual ideas with an empty tray. Each ideology and theology has *some* attractive elements. You could pick and choose whatever parts and pieces appealed to you and leave the rest. Even though I haven't taken this route, I'm tempted by it, drawn to it.

The spiritual cafeteria is perfect for people like me who don't like to be categorized. No one group would impose their beliefs on me. I wouldn't be categorized, I'd be customized.

Another approach I haven't chosen, but harbors some appeal, is the *I'm a spiritual person in general* path. This kind of spirituality embraces whatever comes along that seems spiritual but it gives no definition, no parameters for that spirituality. I can relate to this because spiritual life seemingly does defy definition. Every attempt to describe God is provisional. Irony and paradox permeate spiritual life.

Still I resist these ways of spiritual living. I resist because with these approaches *I* end up being the definition and center of the spirituality. Hey, I've tried playing God. It didn't work out that well.

Did you see the movie *Bruce Almighty*? God offers down-on-his-luck newscaster Bruce the chance to be God for a time. Bruce accepts and then goes on to use his new power in some twisted ways. He sabotages a coworker's live news broadcast to get a promotion. He secretly increases the size of his girlfriend's breasts. He causes the wind to blow a woman's skirt up. He even gets his dog to sit on the toilet. Somewhere in the middle of the humor and the silliness, the movie invites a great question: *If you were God, what would you do?* Bruce ultimately determines he doesn't have what it takes to be God. I came to the same conclusion for myself. That's part of the reason I've chosen a spirituality where I'm not the definition or center of my own spiritual life. I don't think I'm equipped for that.

The disciplines I discuss in this chapter have allowed me to sink roots deeply into spirituality. They've connected me to a God who calls, woos, seduces, overwhelms, but never forces or assaults. It is a spirituality that is practiced alone *and* in community. It is concrete and mystical.

I come to this spirituality with the hope that I will grow roots; that I will really connect with God in a way that can make a difference. Yet even after I make a personal decision to know and follow God, well, the beauty that I believe lives somewhere inside me doesn't always flow into my lifestyle. Where are the results? Can I hope for more than a warm feeling?

A visitor from America was admiring the beauty of an English country estate. She asked the gardener, "How do you make these beautiful British lawns?" The gardener answered, "Oh, you just roll them for two hundred years."[2] I want my life to grow into everything possible, but it takes a good bit of discipline to keep rolling the lawn. I understand that there is no such thing as *instant roots*. Have you noticed that January television and magazines seem to be filled with ads for weight loss? Marketing folks know that we've made New Year's resolutions to lose weight. So in January they give us the "new," "easy," and "instant" weight loss pill, diet, or exercise. Look! You can go from an overweight slob to a sexy, desirable model in *two weeks with no effort or pain*. This advertising must be working—it appears every January like clockwork. Some (or is it many?) of us believe what they're selling really can do what it claims.

I'm not selling *Insta-Root*. You can't go from a tumbleweed existence to a rooted, connected life in two weeks without pain or effort. Root growing can be slow. (There's that time theme again.) You'll encounter painful experiences. You must exert some effort. The kind of habits I want to encourage you to take up will not have instant results. They work more like glaciers than earthquakes. Earthquakes move with sudden violent force. Glaciers inch their way across the landscape, but as they move they carve beauty and deposit richness.

These disciplines put you in a position to connect with God so He can make your life lush. The disciplines themselves can't create something thick and rich in your life (that's the work of God's grace), but they do help you sink deep roots into God—they help you to enjoy a meaningful spiritual life. I suggest these disciplines because they've worked for me, for pilgrims of old, and for ancient travelers of Scripture. Go ahead, they're cheering you on.

Prayer

The vast majority of people in the United States believe in a God who responds to prayer. Most people also pray from time to time. A lesser percentage pursue prayer intentionally as a means to connect with God so He can transform their lives. For those who've chosen this path, prayer is the breathing of spiritual life, the most basic expression of "aliveness" in a relationship with God.

We use the word *prayer* to describe our communication with God. As with human-to-human communication, one of the keys to a healthy dialogue is honesty. We miss the point of prayer if we preoccupy our thoughts with attempts to be poetic or say just the right words or toss in a few "Thee's" or "Thou's." The kind of prayer that grows deep spiritual roots flows out of a raw, gut-level candor. Faking it with God accomplishes nothing. It's not like you can fool God or impress Him with your words. Honest prayer gives God direct access to your heart.

Early communities of faith preserved some prayers that are so honest they might shock readers. Listen to some of these prayers:

God, God . . . my God!
Why did you dump me miles from nowhere?
Doubled up with pain, I call to God all the day long. No
answer. Nothing.
I keep at it all night, tossing and turning.

And you! Are you indifferent, above it all?
(Psalm 22:1-3, MSG)

You walked off and left us, and never looked back.
God, how could you do that?
(Psalm 74:1, MSG)

GOD, don't shut me out;
Don't give me the silent treatment, oh God . . .
My God! I've had it with them! Blow them away!
(Psalm 83:1,13, MSG)

Do you pray that honestly? Maybe you've thought you shouldn't say those kinds of things to *God*. God *invites* us to bring our true selves in prayer. Spiritual roots grow in the soil of authenticity.

Prayer also means listening to God. The roots of our spirituality gain depth when we take time to listen in prayer. We present ourselves before God, we still our minds and hearts, and in the quiet, we invite God to say or do whatever God wants to say or do. This aspect of prayer requires time and quiet.

We usually feel uncomfortable with silence. Test me on this: Turn off the TV, the radio—go and sit in a noiseless room. If you're like many Americans, you may start to feel nervous. Without Ross or Rachel or Brokaw or Rather or Springsteen or Bono filling in the silence, we are essentially alone. It can be scary to face ourselves . . . alone. Noise provides a buffer between who we think we are—and who we are, *really*. The quiet forces us to consider the truth—and gives us an opportunity to speak honestly with God.

Spiritual roots often remain shallow not only because of the noise, but also because of our impatience. As we sit in the quiet, thoughts of what we ought to be doing flood our minds. When we resist the urge to leave the silence to catch up on laundry, make a phone call, or get back to cleaning the garage, our roots move deeper. It's important to stay in the quiet long enough to actually encounter who we are and to encounter God. That's the key.

This kind of prayer approaches God as more than just a cosmic Santa Claus. Have you ever treated God that way? You hop up onto God's lap when you want something, speak or whisper your requests, hop off again, and immediately begin acting as if God doesn't even exist—until you need something else. Entertainer Flip Wilson once said, "I'm going to pray. Does anybody want anything?" Maybe that's funny (maybe not), but it's certainly not the best way to grow spiritual roots.

How are your roots growing through prayer? Are you meeting God in the silence with who you really are? Are you allowing time to hear God's voice? If *right now* isn't a good time for quiet solitude, plan a time. How much time do you need? Start with something you can realistically do. Is thirty minutes too much? Start with fifteen. Sit in a comfortable chair. Tell God how you feel and what is happening in your life. Sure, He already knows—but He wants *you* to tell Him. Invite God into the space you're occupying. If you don't have much to say, that's okay. Listen. Don't cut your time short to get on with the noisy tasks of the day.

Plan your life so you can come back to this kind of prayer over and over. You'll want to practice this discipline several times a week, perhaps even make it a daily activity. Health experts tell us that to improve our health we need to physically exercise for about thirty minutes, three times a week. A similar commitment will improve the health of our spiritual roots. Think of the Grand Canyon. The Colorado River didn't carve that out in a day. People drive for hours, days even, to experience the awesome beauty of this natural wonder. That same kind of beauty can live in you. And it begins with opening your life through prayer to God.

Journaling

Journaling has taken an important place in my life, in part because it became a way to express prayer. I like to think of journaling as keeping a diary for my soul. I usually start by writing what I'm thinking or feeling. I may write concerning a particular problem. I may respond to something in my life that's going well. As with prayer, I try to express these things honestly.

As I journal my experiences and feelings, my writing often becomes a prayer. Sometimes these are prayers of complaint—*God, I don't like this.* Sometimes they're prayers of thanksgiving—*God, You are so good to me.* And sometimes they're prayers of supplication—*God, I need You to do something.* Sometimes they're combinations of all three. Here's an example:

> *I'm struggling so much right now with friendships, family, work, everything. Nothing seems to be working right. Why do I have these times? Life seems to be so up and down, top to bottom. I wish it were more balanced. Why can't I just be more constant, consistent?*
>
> *God, I think You care about me, but I don't feel it very much right now. I struggle to live like You are real when I don't feel Your presence. Why can't You just make me feel Your presence all the time? I'm sure my life would feel more balanced—more evened out—if I could feel Your presence.*
>
> *I feel sort of silly complaining with all I have to be thankful for. All of the things I seem to be struggling with are small compared to the experiences of so many*

*people. I have such high expectations. I'm not sorry for
the expectations. I like them high. I guess I need help
in how to accept less than I expect while keeping high
expectations.*

When I take time to journal, I force myself to clarify what
I think and feel. The puzzle pieces come together. Journaling
brings things into focus.

Journaling also adds a new perspective, a perspective that
comes from personal reflection instead of the noisy opinions
of the world we inhabit the rest of the day. And multiple perspectives are important. If we only see from only one angle, we
limit our ability to see creative solutions to problems. The more
perspectives we have, the more options we find.

When you journal, allow your personality to come out. Some
people structure their journaling around an outline such as:

1. What is happening in my life?
2. How do I feel about that?
3. What is my response?

Others just start writing and let the words fall onto the
page as they think them. You may want to use your computer
for journaling, but I really like the tactile nature of writing in a
book. I chose a black suede book with lined pages. How might
you approach journaling? Choose a system that works for you.

Worship

While journaling is a solitary discipline, prayer can be experienced both in solitude *and* with others in community. Praying
with a group gives you a spiritual connection with others as well
as with God. Even times of group silence can bring a powerful
spiritual experience.

This communal prayer is one aspect of a larger discipline:

worship. Simply stated, in worship, a spiritual community comes together to treat God like God. Worship can take place in a traditional church setting, with friends around a dining room table, around a campfire, and just about anywhere else. Worship is more than prayer. It's more than God-honoring music. And it's more than listening to a sermon. The only ingredients you really need to experience worship are a group of people seeking God's truth or presence and time to seek. But we're talking about disciplines in this chapter, and that means we ought to consider one more ingredient: regular participation (or consistency in practicing communal worship).

I'd like you to consider a few things as you look for a place to build a habit of communal worship. Some worship settings are more helpful in growing roots than others. Look for a church or gathering that not only speaks about the value of community, but one that practices community. There are probably more than a few churches in your neighborhood where you could sit unnoticed each Sunday. Where you could attend for months before other attendees introduce themselves or invite you to coffee. The ability to attend church in cloaking mode may sound appealing, but let's not forget your goal. You're not looking for anonymity in worship—you're looking for connection. Remember those roots you're trying to grow? I discovered this kind of community at a worship gathering in Houston.

I participated in the Sunday worship gathering that began at six in the evening. I had planned to eat dinner with one of the church leaders after the worship was over, but when 7:15 rolled around and the service ended, the gathering continued. For an hour or more I sat along the side of the room and watched. All across the room people talked in small groups of four to eight people. Most people circulated from one circle to another. As I sat on the side watching, people would come to introduce themselves. Still, I felt free to sit on the sidelines, enter into conversation, or join a circle. I saw a few people talking seriously with one another. You could tell that they were talking about something really important. Something special was happening. These people didn't just "do time" at worship and then rush off to do their own thing. This was truly a community.

Community is key in deciding where to worship. But it's also important to choose a gathering where you are free to be you. This goes beyond choosing a certain style of music. Of course, if you resonate with the long tradition of hymns and organ music, you'll want to seek that kind of worship gathering. If you enjoy a more contemporary style, try out contemporary churches or worship gatherings. What I'm really getting at is finding a worship gathering where you feel free to worship according to the way you like to express yourself. Do you enjoy clapping and singing along with lively music? Do you connect with liturgy and tradition? Do you like the freedom to express your emotions? Do you like to wear comfortable jeans and a sweatshirt? Would you rather your experience feel more like creating art than attending a lecture?

It can be difficult to get started in a worship gathering. Some people feel intimidated just showing up. Are you wearing the right clothes? Will people corner you with questions you can't answer? Will the pastor call attention to all the visitors and make you stand up and wave?

And then there's the baggage. Perhaps your experience with church in the past wasn't so good. Or maybe you're just skeptical about the value of organized worship gatherings.

I have a friend who says his first worship experience happened in a parking lot. He had decided to worship with others who met for worship in a movie theater. When my friend drove into the parking lot he began to feel really nervous. He just couldn't bring himself to walk into the theater. He had watched movies there, but suddenly when the theater was hosting a worship gathering, he couldn't walk in. So, he sat in the parking lot and watched the other people walk through the doors. After repeating this parking lot experience a few times, he finally mustered the courage to enter the theater. Today he is a regular participant in this spiritual community and has come to greatly value the worship gathering. Maybe you know a similar anxiety. Move through the nervousness and take that risk to find a community where you can worship just as you are.

There are other disciplines, too. I haven't taken the space to describe spiritual reading, practicing service and hospitality, or fasting. These are all excellent pursuits. I encourage you to learn about and experiment with these as well. Find what works best for you.

Now that I'm closing this chapter, I want to repeat something I've already said. (It's that important.) These disciplines in themselves won't grow roots or change your life. They will bring you to a place where you can get what you need to grow spiritual roots. This reminds me of gardening. I really enjoy gardening. I like planning where everything will go, tilling the soil, and carefully planting the seeds with the correct depth and spacing. I like getting my hands dirty.

After all the planning and preparation, I wait. I look every few days to see if the seeds have sprouted and pushed through the soil, but I can't make the seeds grow. While I play a role in helping the seeds prepare for growth, it's ultimately not up to me if the seeds grow or not. I also can't make my spiritual roots grow. I *can* place myself before God in prayer. I *can* honestly express myself through journaling. I *can* participate in a worship gathering. And God will do the rest.

I have described the path I take to growing spiritual roots. I confess that I have not arrived at the goal. I travel this path with you and it's a lifelong journey. As we walk this path we will sink deep spiritual roots. We will feel connected. And we will begin to leave behind the tumbleweed life.

Chapter Eight

PLANT A FAMILY

s you've probably noticed by now, the family I grew up with was far from the epitome of a "healthy family." While I was still young, my immediate family fractured. Then all my connections to extended family began to crack and eventually ruptured. With my family splintered, I chose other things to occupy the important places in my life. A spiritual vacuum left me without the needed spiritual resources. My value system became pragmatic—I opted for whatever worked for me in the moment. I struggled to find a place to hang on, and in the process I lost myself.

The tumbleweed life.

As a seventeen-year-old I made a crucial decision. You might not think seventeen-year-olds make life-altering decisions (particularly ones that stick), but I did. I decided to do something that would make a palpable difference in my life. I had just begun to pursue spirituality. For the first time in a long time, I found a group of people with whom I could grow real, lasting friendships. And I made a significant decision about this concept called "family."

I decided that I would one day have a family much different from the one I grew up in. Now, I know lots of teenagers say something like that. "It won't be like this when *I'm* the parent." But my decision wasn't so vague. I decided to make a specific commitment to a family that didn't yet exist. I knew I wanted to really love my wife. I determined that I would marry someone I'd love for the rest of our lives. I would be faithful to her. We'd genuinely care for our children. We'd nurture them and teach them how to love others unconditionally.

I even took some practical steps toward that goal of a healthy, happy family. I started listening to a national radio broadcast from Focus on the Family. This may sound odd for a teenager. Okay, it *is* odd. But I wanted more than anything to have a happy, emotionally healthy family. I also started reading books on family life. I began living out a commitment to the family that didn't yet exist.

In college I met Lisa. My usual dating rhythm was to grow interested in a girl, date her for a little while, then grow tired of the relationship. Something different happened in my relationship with Lisa. I didn't grow tired of this relationship. Instead, the more I knew her the more she intrigued me. She had absolutely captured my attention.

I didn't realize it at the time, but she had roots. Boy, did she have roots, roots so long and thick they could choke you to death. (I mean this in a good way, really.) I guess I have to admit I'm a root man. I needed her sense of rootedness.

After Lisa and I married we made our family a central part of our lives. We probably should've waited longer to have children. We were young and didn't have the money. But we wanted so badly to share our love with children. We realize now that if you have them early, they leave home when you're still young. (Although, some of our friends have told us that they may *never* leave or they may come back again after they leave.) We struggled at times but we never regretted our decisions to focus so much on family. We love celebrating birthdays and Christmas. We've attended countless school programs, dance recitals, and ball games. We've spent too much money on them and worried when we didn't need to worry. And we've loved every minute of it.

That commitment I made at seventeen to my future family was a commitment to grow roots. I didn't know it at the time, but when I was helping my family to establish roots, I was actually growing roots myself. I'm not sure how this happens, but when you plant a family, you end up growing yourself.

Untangling the Family Roots

One of the most enjoyable things I get to do as a pastor is to meet with couples before their marriage ceremony. I usually meet with them a half-dozen times over a three-month time period. I encourage couples to think about their marriage relationship and not just the ceremony. Typically, engaged couples spend tons of time, energy, and money on a thirty-minute ceremony and very little time, energy, or money on the actual marriage. That first thirty minutes turns out to be the easiest part. It's the next thirty years that are the real challenge. So I challenge them to think about how they'll negotiate actually living together as a married couple.

One of the primary topics I get them to talk about is how they relate to their parents. A healthy sense of family connectedness can provide a good setting from which to sprout a new branch of the family tree. Many newly married couples want or need help from extended family. Becoming an extension of a family heritage with healthy relationships can set them up for success.

Family roots can mean so much, but an unhealthily root-bound family of origin can also choke a new marriage. Consider the story of Steve and Jan. They had been married for about six years and had two children. While Steve worked in his father's business and Jan worked elsewhere out of the home, Steve's mother took care of the children. Steve's parents took responsibility for buying the children's clothes and even their Christmas presents year after year. Do you see a problem developing?

Steve's mother admitted that she would tell Jan how to handle the children—everything from discipline to health care. She told Jan that since she paid for everything she had the right to demand a certain kind of care for the children. With this kind of pressure, Jan had grown bitter toward Steve's parents. The bitterness toward Steve's parents ultimately led to feelings of bitterness toward Steve. Jan tried to talk to Steve about her feelings, but in the end, Steve wasn't willing to draw a boundary for his parents.

I tell this story to every engaged couple I meet with. Usually, though not always, they say, "My parents would *never* do anything like that." I talk to some of these same couples again a few years into the marriage, just when one or both partners are at their wit's end due to overinvolved or manipulative parents.

Connected, Not Consumed

One of the keys to growing a family with strong roots is knowing the difference between being connected with your parents and being consumed by them. You are *consumed* by parents if you count on their roots as your own, if you depend solely on them for your rootedness. You are *connected* with parents and other extended family if you can call upon them for guidance when needed but don't feel compelled to follow that guidance if you disagree. The roots you grow are your own. Plant them in a soil of your choosing.

Since the line between "connected" and "consumed" is often quite thin, I want to give you a few suggestions that will build the former and reduce the impact of the latter.

Start Your Own Family Traditions

The Hilburns will always have a real tree at Christmas. We usually go as a family to choose the tree and every year we remember all the other years we've picked out a tree. There was a brief season when we didn't have a real tree—when we thought our young daughter might have been allergic to them. That's one of the first memories we share when we're picking out a new real tree. We also remember the year we got a tree when it was hot and dry in the Houston area. The people who owned the tree farm gave us a really good deal on the tree we chose because it was practically dead before we even cut it down. It looked awful. That was the "ugliest tree year." We recall the prettiest tree year from a time when we lived in Wisconsin. They grow real Christmas trees there. We took a sleigh ride out into the Christmas tree farm and cut down a beautiful tree in the snow.

I know, for a lot less money and hassle we could purchase an artificial tree—even one with all the lights already in place. But that's not what we do. We have too much fun retelling these stories, arguing over which tree to get, and taking photos after it's all decorated. The tradition helps us all grow roots. This past year Josh, our youngest, suggested we get a Christmas fern. Leave it to Josh to think of something wacky, but kind of cool. We stuck with the tree.

The fact that we choose a real tree isn't what's important in this story. It's all about building traditions. You might have the very same kind of "we always do it this way" experience with an artificial tree. Or even a fern.

Look for ways to start traditions in your family that stem from the traditions you grew up with. If you had a pretty good childhood (and sometimes, even if you didn't), you might find some things are worth continuing. Some traditions hold as much value as any family heirloom.

When Bob was growing up, his family traditionally vacationed at a mountain cabin. He remembers these vacations often and with great fondness. They would swim in the cool lake water. The entire family would hike to the top of the mountain and picnic there while looking at the most beautiful view they would see all year.

When Bob's children were small, he took them to the mountains. He and his wife looked forward to a great time together, but as it turned out, Bob's children hated the mountains. Wouldn't you know it? But they love the beach. Now they rent the same beach house every year. They've gotten to know some of the locals who live near their rental and they get together every year during vacation. Bob's children plan to come to the beach for vacation as long as they live. Of course their children will probably prefer the desert. The point is that Bob has been flexible enough to take a tradition from his childhood and mold it to fit his current family. They all grow roots because of it.

Holidays provide great opportunities to start traditions. Include some kind of ritual as part of your holiday celebration. Attend a Christmas Eve church service. Pray together at Thanksgiving. Visit a fireworks show on the Fourth of July. Read Martin Luther King Jr.'s "I Have A Dream" speech on Martin Luther King Jr. Day. Rituals like these add meaning to your traditions. You can also build traditions around other seasonal events, such as sporting events (Super Bowl, World Series) or birthdays.

Document Your Family Life

Photographs are a miracle of technology. Maybe I'm simple-minded but I'm amazed that a little box can produce a visual representation of any given moment. You can use this miracle of technology to grow family roots.

I have very few pictures of myself before the age of twenty-one. Most of the photos I have are school pictures. No one took time to photograph important moments in my life. That may not seem like a big deal. Maybe it isn't. But think of what you could do if you did have lots of pictures. You could pull out a shoebox of photos and sit on the floor with your family to look through them. You'd pull out one picture and say, "Look. That's me. Look at my hair! What was I thinking?" Someone else would pick up a picture and say, "I remember that shirt. I thought I was so cool." You would remember the moment, you would revisit the event. Pictures are like there-and-back-again time machines. They can make you feel familiar feelings, hear familiar sounds, and even smell familiar smells.

I think it's important to give your family those there-and-back-again moments. Photos do this. So does artwork. We have kept most of Josh's artwork. I know, everybody keeps those mystery art pieces for the fridge. But for Josh this is special. Josh is a creative genius. I'm not saying this just because I'm his dad. Honest! We want Josh to always know that he is a creative genius. We also want him to know that we have and always will value this unique part of who he is.

When our middle child, Caleb, was born, my wife started his baby book. Over the years, Lisa took the time to write down things that Caleb did or said—things that helped to define who he was becoming. If you read about Caleb from his earliest years, you will discover a recurring theme. You'll read about him playing with all kinds of balls. You'll discover how Caleb likes to wrestle and have fun with his dad. To this day, whatever Caleb does, he does with a sense of playfulness and fun. This is an important part of who Caleb is. One day when Caleb is not so sure about who he is, when he doubts his heart, he can read what Lisa wrote. He can be reminded that God has written fun and play into his heart.

Teach Your Family Values

Embrace specific values as a family. What things are important to you that you want to pass along? I suggest you separate the important stuff from those things that may be nothing more than your personal preferences. For example, learning to accept people for who they are without judging is a value worth handing down, but keeping your room spotless is probably more of a preference.

As much as you'd like it to happen, you probably won't pass along all of your preferences and values. (Did you keep all that your parents tried to imprint on you?) Determine what's most important. List only those things you would like to outlive you. What are the half-dozen things you consider nonnegotiable for rooted living? I'll give you a list to help you get started:

Faith

Self-Respect

Honesty

Family Commitment

Creativity

Respect for Creation

Friendships

Serving Others

Positive Outlook

One of the best definitions of *values* I've heard is "the things you are willing to pay for." Values cost time and money and effort—and they often involve sacrifice. For example, if you choose "respect for creation" as one of your values, you may donate money to an environmental cause, you may spend time and effort recycling or composting, and, if you live in Texas like I do, you may decide to sacrifice the "yard of the month" award from the Garden Club and instead grow native grasses and plants that don't require excessive watering.

Planting a family means more than just deciding on values; it means living out those values. Don't embrace values as a family unless you're willing to practice them.

One of the best ways to communicate your values is to collect and tell family stories that reinforce them. Do you have a story of what Grandma or Uncle Frank once did, or even something from another branch of the family tree? These stories can become powerful family scripts for future generations. In addition to your own family stories, look to Scripture. Adopt the Bible stories that communicate your values as your own and pass these along as well.

Have you ever thought of using a proverb as a communication tool? Proverbs are simple ways to pass on wisdom. They can be easily and often repeated. You probably know how these proverbs end:

A bird in the hand is worth . . .

Haste makes . . .

If you don't have something good to say . . .

Did your parents or grandparents ever use proverbs? My dad often said, "If a job is worth doing, it is worth doing right." My mom often said, "Lying is just like stealing." See, I still remember. Your family will also remember whatever proverbs you create and use. Brainstorm some proverbs together with family members. Personalize them. Print them out and tack them on a mirror or the refrigerator. Or even create a plaque with your proverbs.

Proverbs 13:22 says, "A good man leaves an inheritance for his children's children." While you are considering the land, house, or other valuables you may leave for your children and grandchildren, ask yourself about the spiritual heritage you will leave. Your children may liquidate the property and spend their inheritance money before it ever gets to your grandchildren, but a spiritual heritage can last for generations.

You may want to create a spiritual will. If you are not sure how to get started on a spiritual will, read some of the blessings from one generation to the next in the Old Testament. Read Genesis 49, where Jacob blesses his sons; Deuteronomy 33, which records Moses blessing the people of Israel; and 1 Kings 2, where David spoke to his son Solomon about carrying on the family heritage. Write a will that expresses the values you desire to pass down to your children. Then live out those values each day.

Involve Your Extended Family

Family roots often grow stronger if you keep your branch connected to the rest of the family tree. As much as you are able (and as much as it seems appropriate), keep relationships alive with aunts, uncles, cousins, and grandparents. Send them photos. Make phone calls on birthdays. Visit them on vacation.

Invite extended family to special events. A ten-year-old can have lots of fun playing on a basketball team. He can learn about teamwork and grow in confidence. But if six or eight family members and relatives cheer from the stands, he gains something more—a heightened sense that people care about him. Making straight A's on a report card represents a noteworthy accomplishment. But if Grandma and Grandpa come over for dinner and bring a cake to celebrate, it's not just about accomplishment anymore, it's about feeling valued. You can't have too many people cheering for you or celebrating you.

If you have children who don't know their extended family, you may want to rethink how you interact with aunts, uncles, cousins, parents, and grandparents. It's your responsibility to give your children opportunities to connect. You may conclude that some extended family connections would be more detrimental than helpful. That's certainly valid. But don't overlook the simple ways you can connect, even with those you may not agree with. Write letters. Send family updates by e-mail. Pass along those photos. As much as it is possible and good, give your children the chance to entangle their roots with extended family.

Planting Without Children

If you don't have your own children, you can grow family-like roots by investing in the lives of nonrelatives. You won't need to look far to find someone who could use a mentor, a "big brother" or "big sister," or simply a friend.

As a sixteen-year-old, I had very few positive connections with adults. About this time I got to know a man named Lynn. He was the youth minister at a local church. For some reason he took a personal interest in me. At the time I couldn't see how Lynn benefited from mentoring me—I wasn't a member of his church and I wasn't going to become a member of his church. But now I see that this relationship not only changed the direction of my life, it also deepened Lynn's life.

Lynn has since told me how his mentoring relationship with me brought him a sense of renewal. As a cynical sixteen-year-old I would never have listened to someone whose lifestyle wasn't consistent with what they were saying. Everything Lynn sought to grow in my life had to be growing in his life as well. I was willing to listen to and learn from Lynn because what he told me was validated by how he lived.

Lynn is not related to me. But he planted something in my life that continues to grow today; it even impacts my children and the roots *they're* growing. I know a half-dozen people who today are growing rooted families because of Lynn's influence. Keep in mind, to help someone else grow roots you can't just unpack stale ideas. You can't offer an artificial plant as a pattern. Like Lynn, you must be growing real roots yourself.

Keep On Planting

After your children are grown and on their own you can continue planting family roots. Perhaps someday you'll have grandchildren. Grandparents have incredible root-growing opportunities. Think about it. You may get to be involved in your grandchildren's lives for thirty or forty years. You may also be graced with the opportunity to help introduce great-grandchildren to this world.

Ed and Francine chose to be involved in the lives of their grandchildren. With the first grandchild, they began a tradition of vacationing together at their lake cabin. As more grandchildren joined the extended family, they joined in the annual summer trip. After a few years someone started calling these vacations "Granny Camp."

Ed and Francine were concerned that their children and grandchildren might, over time, move away and miss out on getting to know each other. Granny Camp gave the kids a chance to build close connections with each other. While unstructured, Granny Camp did have its priorities. One of the main priorities was fun. Every child needs a chance to play and get dirty without getting in trouble for it. After a day of grimy fun, all the campers would take a bath in the lake because the sewer system at the cabin couldn't handle the cavalcade of potential bathers. Anyway, the lake was more fun. Grandparents are especially good with "fun."

Some years they would organize Granny Camp around a theme. One year they all became soldiers. Upon arrival everyone was issued a backpack, a helmet, and a canteen. For lunch they took safaris to the top of the hill. Another year they celebrated their Native American heritage. Campers' tents became teepees. Kids each constructed a bow and arrow. Everyone adopted a Native American name for the week. They roasted hot dogs over a fire in front of the teepees and each person would eat the hot dog they roasted, whether cold or burned.

Francine would fix breakfast and serve it on the deck. After breakfast every day, Francine took time to talk to the grandchildren about faith. She prized this time. She wanted her grandchildren to hear directly from her what she believed, what she valued about her faith.

The grandchildren continue to gather at Ed and Francine's home from time to time. They phone regularly. One of the boys brought friends for spring break. Not the usual spring break trip I would guess. Some of the grandchildren talk to Ed and Francine about things they don't talk to anybody else about. You know, parents just don't understand some things. Ed and Francine say, "That's what grandparents are for."

If Granny Camp interests you, Ed and Francine will be glad to tell you all about it. It has played such an important role in their lives. They have filled several photo albums with the memories. If you don't want to look through the photos, you can watch the video. When the grandkids come to visit these days they watch the video together and remember. How much do you think that video is worth? Bill Gates couldn't afford it. How do you get a video that valuable? You plant a family and then *keep on planting.*

Family roots can take you a long way. They took George W. Bush to the White House. You may think George W. didn't get enough votes to become president or he may not be smart enough to be president. You may think his political ideas may not be right for our country. Even so, he has presidential roots.

The symbol of these roots was introduced in 1943 on an airstrip in Corpus Christi, Texas. A young Navy pilot has just graduated and is standing with his parents to say good-bye as he leaves for his assignment. Quietly, the father takes two gold cuff links from his pocket. He passes them to his son. This simple act gives courage and direction. The young man will remember this moment when his plane is shot down and when he makes difficult decisions behind closed doors as head of the CIA. These cuff links will anchor him when he becomes president of the United States of America.

A day comes when this man knows that he can no longer hold on to the cuff links. Now it's his turn to give them away. He packages them with a note. George W. hardly notices when the cuff links and note are given to him on the day of his inauguration as governor of Texas in 1995. During an inauguration prayer breakfast sermon George W. reaches into his pocket to find the gift and the note. In part, the note says, "These cuff links are my most treasured possession. . . . I want you to have them now. . . . Now, it's your turn."

We can give our families something that will take them further than intelligence or ability ever could. We can give them roots.

A FEW THOUGHTS FOR PASTORS AND OTHER SPIRITUAL LEADERS

Pastors, mentors, and other spiritual leaders stand at the edge of a new frontier: a culture that has opened the door to spiritual questions. For many years, spiritual questions took a backseat to science. More and more people are determining that science can't answer all of their questions. Why is it that science could send us to the moon but couldn't keep the space shuttle from exploding? Twice. Do you remember when to be healthy you were supposed to eat a low-fat diet? Now the fat doesn't matter. Bacon for breakfast, lunch, and dinner. Yum. Now it's all about the carbs. Sure, science helps us all, but it only offers provisional answers.

People also used to believe that education and reason could solve all of society's ills. We've learned that smarter people don't necessarily become better people. Just because we own more tools doesn't mean we know how to use them. More information and education is available to our culture than ever before. Have things gotten better? Are we better people? Are families better off than they were a hundred years ago? What happened to the inevitable progress?

Science and education and reason have not disappeared. They've just scooted over a little to make room at the table for spirituality. People are suddenly interested in what spiritual leaders have to say. People are recognizing the need to discover what that means to be spiritual and yearning to know how to develop their spiritual lives. We need to be ready to take a seat at the table to be part of the discussion.

Authentic Roots

Spiritual leaders today must do their work from authentic roots. No longer is the title given by an institution such as the church enough to qualify us as leaders. Did you see the movie *Secondhand Lions*? You may have missed this one. Maybe you thought it would be too predictable. It's the story of an unstable mother who drops her young boy off to live with his cranky old uncles. What could possibly surprise us with this sort of movie? The boy and his cranky uncles won't get along at first, then they'll develop a friendship laced with humor, and everything will be tied up with a warm, fuzzy ending. Right? Well, to some degree, yes. But there is so much more in this movie.

A pivotal quote in the movie comes from Hub, the uncle played by Robert Duval. Walter, the nephew played by Haley Joel Osment, wants to know if the fantastic stories told by his uncles (stories that explain their great wealth) are true, if they really happened exactly as they'd been told. Hub explains that it doesn't matter if they're factually true. Instead he tells Walter that the key question to ask about any story is, "Is it worth believing in?"

But the movie isn't over yet. When Walter's mother and her new boyfriend arrive on the scene with a different explanation of how his uncles gained their fortune—bank robbery—he must decide between two versions of truth. His mother's version seems more factual. But the uncles' version of the truth resonates with his heart.

Which story is worth believing? Walter makes his decision partly based on the trustworthiness of those telling the story. Which storytellers have Walter's interest at heart and which want something for themselves? Which storytellers would Walter want to follow? One of these stories will define Walter's life.

Welcome to decision making in the emerging culture.

For several centuries spiritual leaders have sold themselves as dispensers of truth because they have the facts. In emerging culture, some think the facts are only a piece of the truth puzzle—and sometimes are even meaningless. The question being posed these days is, *Do we have a story worth believing in?* Other questions coming from emerging culture include:

- Who is the storyteller?
- Is the storyteller's life consistent with what he or she is saying?
- Do the storytellers actually care for me or are they in this for themselves?
- Where will this story take me and will I be glad I lived out of this story?

If we want to operate as spiritual leaders today we can't rely on position or title to give us credibility. We must be rooted. We must deeply care for people. We must demonstrate the kind of life people can expect to experience if they choose to live out of the story we tell.

But there's more. We also need integrity.

Integrity

I hesitate to even use the word *integrity* because it seems to have lost its, well, integrity. When I say that spiritual leaders need integrity I mean that what appears to be true must also be true to the core.

Some of us have become like salesmen who have learned to make good presentations but can't deliver on the promises. We promise an ocean and deliver a thimbleful of water instead. We need to change that. We need to deliver on the things we promise by pressing our lives into the lives of others.

I recently sat with a friend in his office having a cup of

coffee. Between us was a small table and beside the table, a large pot with a sagging, yellowing plant. The once-green leaves were fading. The vitality of the plant had withered without water. My friend apologized for the condition of his plant.

He said, "Well, at least you can tell it's real. No one would make an artificial plant that looks like this." My friend may not have a green thumb, but he's right. The plant was only half alive, but at least it was alive. Artificial plants may never turn yellow or droop, but they also never grow roots, experience the surging life that water and soil provide, or reproduce. As a spiritual leader you have a choice. You can artificially arrange your appearance to look just right or you can focus on growing roots, allowing life to flow through you, and reproducing yourself in others. If you choose the second option, expect to have dry seasons too. But remember: Half-alive is better than not alive at all. Integrity, when lived out in real time, shows up in green leaves *and* yellow.

Openness

Some spiritual leaders never impress the contour of their lives onto others because they don't let people get close enough to make an impression. Think about the person who impacted your life most deeply. If you're like me, this person helped shape the important channels in your life by granting you a "backstage pass" to their own life.

Some of us build walls because we fear getting hurt. Our experience has taught us that the world is a dangerous place, so we construct barricades of protection. We try to keep the dangerous people from getting close enough to cause fatal damage. These decisions are almost unconscious. Our defensive posture has become a reflex response triggered by anyone who gets too close.

The walls we build around ourselves are constructed with various materials. Some of us display an aloof air of perfection. We wear a veneer that says to the world, "I don't need you." We offer help to needy people. We walk into *their* world. But the gate that allows access into our world is closely guarded. Do we still accomplish some good? Sure. But the people we lead need more than lectures, good advice, handouts, and a distant example. They need to see authenticity up close.

Self-Definition

Leading is hard work. It requires a complex matrix of skills. Some of us have learned these leadership skills—we've read all the books—but haven't stopped to consider that leadership skills are *secondary* to who the leader is.

Tumbleweeds who become spiritual leaders can struggle to define themselves. We're accustomed to allowing outside pressures to define us. We tend to lead by the Jell-O method. We just form to whatever mold we are poured into. Is that leadership?

Your best leadership days will be those when you define yourself authentically from the inside out. Those days when you know who you are, warts and all. When you lead from there, you invite others to walk closely with you. You will be a good leader not because of your position, or because you've mastered certain techniques, but because you are authentically alive.

One final thought. An authentically alive leader is far from perfect. You know this, you've looked in the mirror and seen yellowing leaves often enough. Some people will see your imperfections and be disillusioned. You're right; the world can be a dangerous place. But those sometimes-yellow leaves make you a better leader. A compellingly, refreshingly honest leader. Yes, there's a risk in being authentic. As a leader you must choose to live in a world of risk to get the reward.

What's the reward? Building God-honoring roots in others. *And* in yourself.

And that's no small thing.

READER'S GUIDE

Use these questions to spark discussion in a small-group setting or with a friend.

1. What was your emotional response to the introduction as the author described the "tumbleweed life"? What might this say about your own experience?

2. Where did you grow the deepest roots in your growing-up years? What made those roots strong?

3. In what ways do you connect with TV shows such as *Friends, Cheers,* and *The Andy Griffith Show*? What other TV shows draw you in? What, if any, connection do you see between your interest in these shows and your upbringing?

4. What would your "Mayberry" look like?

5. Describe your tumbleweed experience. What aspects of a tumbleweed life do you relate to most?

6. In what ways do you see yourself compelled to seek community? What challenges does that present?

7. Where are you "connected" today? Where do you seek deeper connections?

8. What does your "lonely wail of the tumbleweed" sound like?

9. How have distrust, alienation, and feelings of insignificance affected your ability to grow roots?

10. What good memories provide you with glimpses of hope?

11. Which of the windstorms most impact your ability to connect? Are these things you can change? How would you do that?

12. How do you respond when someone asks you, "Where are you from?" What does that say about your roots? What would you like to be able to say?

13. Describe some practical ways you can discover your heritage. What are your fears about doing this? What are your expectations?

14. How might you go about "recovering what you can" from your past without getting stuck in the painful stuff?

15. When have you felt the most connected to your heart? What does it look like for you to live from your heart?

16. How might you respond to Jesus if, like Bartimaeus, He asked you, "What do you want?"

17. Think of ways you can "decorate your life" and create a space around you that matches who you really are. What are some of these ideas?

18. When in life do you experience "hurry sickness"? How might you go about finding a cure for this behavior?

19. What does your community look like today? What kind of "root system" does it have? How do you want it to change?

20. Routines can be positive or negative factors in developing community. What are some of the positive ways routine can build community in your life?

21. "Giving things time" is a recurring theme in this book. How easy or difficult is it for you to give things time to grow and develop? What can help you better accept the slow process of growing roots?

22. What spiritual disciplines do you practice today? How might you develop new (or improved) disciplines in your spiritual life? Why is this important?

23. When you think about "prayer," what comes to mind? Is this a good way to think about prayer? Explain.

24. If you journal now, how does that help you grow spiritual roots? If you don't, what would you expect to gain from journaling?

25. How does participating in worship help you grow roots? Do you have a community where you can enjoy worship? If not, what steps can you take to find one that matches your needs and desires?

NOTES

Chapter One

1. Archibald Hart, *Me, Myself, & I: How Far Should We Go in Our Search for Self-Fulfillment* (Ann Arbor, Mich.: Vine, 1992), p. 202.
2. Hart, p. 93.
3. Judith Feeney and Patricia Noller, *Adult Attachment* (Thousand Oaks, Calif.: SAGE Publications, 1996), pp. 70-74.
4. Stanley J. Grenz, *Created for Community: Connecting Christian Belief with Christian Living* (Grand Rapids, Mich.: Baker, 1996), pp. 78-79.
5. Grenz, p. 51.
6. Frank W. Abagnale with Stan Redding, *Catch Me If You Can: The Amazing True Story of the Youngest and Most Daring Con Man in the History of Fun and Profit* (New York: Broadway, 2002), p. 5.
7. Abagnale and Redding, p. 289.
8. Lawrence Kohlberg, *Essays on Moral Development, Vol. 2, The Psychology of Moral Development: The Nature and Validity of Moral Stages* (San Francisco: Harper & Row, 1984), pp. 171-203.

Chapter Two

1. Judith S. Wallerstein, Julia M. Lewis & Sandra Blakeslee, *The Unexpected Legacy of Divorce: The 25 Year Landmark Study* (New York: Hyperion, 2000), pp. 3-4,10.
2. Edward Hallowell, *The Childhood Roots of Adult Happiness* (New York: Ballentine, 2002), p. 3.
3. Brent Curtis and John Eldredge, *The Sacred Romance* (Nashville, Tenn.: Thomas Nelson, 1997), p. 16.

Chapter Three

1. Robert D. Putnam, *Bowling Alone: The Collapse and Revival of American Community* (New York: Simon & Schuster, 2000).
2. Putnam, p. 17.
3. Putnam, p. 20.
4. Putnam, p. 31.

5. Putnam, p. 47.
6. Putnam, p. 183.
7. Putnam, p. 193.
8. Putnam, p. 207.
9. Putnam, p. 217.

Chapter Four

1. Leonard I. Sweet, *Aqua Church* (Loveland, Colo.: Group, 1999), pp. 72-73.
2. *Late Night with Conan O'Brien*, NBC, September 18, 2001.
3. H. Leon McBeth, *The Baptist Heritage* (Nashville, Tenn.: Broadman & Holman, 1987), pp. 28-30.

Chapter Five

1. John Ortberg, *The Life You've Always Wanted* (Grand Rapids, Mich.: Zondervan, 2002), p. 83.
2. http://www.drphil.com.
3. http://www.drphil.com.

Chapter Six

1. http://www.humboldtredwoods.org.
2. Edward M. Hallowell, M.D., *Connect: 12 Vital Ties that Open Your Heart, Lengthen Your Life, and Deepen Your Soul* (New York: Pocket Books, a division of Simon & Schuster, 1999), pp. 104-105.
3. Hallowell, p. 108.
4. Hallowell, p. 110.

Chapter Seven

1. Hebrews 12:1, MSG.
2. Leonard I. Sweet, *SoulSalsa* (Grand Rapids, Mich.: Zondervan, 2002), p. 9.

ABOUT THE AUTHOR

Eddie Hilburn spent his growing-up years in Arkansas, Louisiana, and Georgia. By the time he reached twenty-five, he had lived in a small town, a rural community, a mid-sized city, and an urban neighborhood. He still finds himself at home on a ranch, at the corner drug store, or at Starbucks.

As a sixteen-year-old, Eddie encountered the person of Jesus through the life of two friends. This encounter so impacted him that he decided he would follow Jesus regardless of where that led. After graduating from high school in West Monroe, Louisiana, Eddie moved to Marshall, Texas, to attend East Texas Baptist University. He followed his bachelor's degree with a master's degree from Southwestern Baptist Theological Seminary.

While at East Texas Baptist University, Eddie met his wife, Lisa. Lisa's father has been a pastor all of her life. Remarkably, she decided to choose a pastor as her life partner. Eddie and Lisa have three children, Bailey, Caleb, and Joshua.

Along with loving his wife and watching his children grow, Eddie enjoys golfing and gardening. The gardening may be payment for the golfing. After destroying a perfectly manicured fairway, he comes home to attempt recompense by growing a vegetable or flower garden.

Eddie has served God as a youth minister, church planter, and pastor. He currently serves as pastor of First Baptist Church in Frankston, Texas.

"YET MANY OF US WOULD CRY OUT, 'YOU HAVE NO IDEA WHO I AM!' WE'RE WEARING A MASK. DESPITE OUR RELATIONSHIPS, MANY OF US FEEL DESPERATELY ALONE AND DEEPLY UNKNOWN."

-quote taken from *TrueFaced*-

TrueFaced

Bill Thrall, Bruce McNicol, and John Lynch   1-57683-693-2

In this revolutionary book, we discover that the devastating source of defeat is in attempting to hide our unresolved sin issues, keeping us immature unfulfilled. But God's way to an astonishing life begins as we start living as He sees us, standing with him to work on our issues together.

TrueFaced Experience Guide

Bill Thrall, Bruce McNicol, and John Lynch   1-57683-678-9

An eight-week "experience guide" for small groups and individuals to explore the revolutionary concept of allowing ourselves the grace to be real with God and others.

TrueFaced Experience DVD

Bill Thrall, Bruce McNicol, and John Lynch   1-57683-680-0

Take your TrueFaced experience one step further. In this eight-week DVD series, you and your small-group will examine a revolutionary message of grace. Features the dynamic teaching of author John Lynch. Use with the *TrueFaced Experience Guide*.

Visit your local Christian bookstore,
call NavPress at 1-800-366-7788, or log on to www.navpress.com to purchase.

To locate a Christian bookstore near you,
call 1-800-991-7747.

NAVPRESS ®

BRINGING TRUTH TO LIFE

www.navpress.com